JOE PIERI

STORIES FROM A GLASGOW CAFÉ

Foreword by Colin Bell

Neil Wilson Publishing • Glasgow • Scotland

First published by
Neil Wilson Publishing
303a The Pentagon Centre
36 Washington Street
GLASGOW
G3 8AZ
Tel: 0141-221-1117
Fax: 0141-221-5363
E-mail: nwp@cqm.co.uk
http://www.nwp.co.uk/

A catalogue record for this book is
available from the British Library.

ISBN 1-897784-94-5
Typeset in Gill and Joanna
Designed by Mark Blackadder
Printed by WSOY, Finland

CONTENTS

TALES OF *The* SAVOY

FOREWORD
Colin Bell

*I*t's scarcely a century since the first Italian immigrants (if we ignore the Romans) began to arrive in Scotland, yet it would be difficult to exaggerate the impact they have had on our society. On the stage, in the arts, the law, architecture and journalism, Scots of Italian descent have achieved not just success, but the highest accolades: yet the rest of us still perhaps think first of the caterers – Lord Forte, Valvona & Crolla, and innumerable chippers and ice-cream shops, rather than Paolozzi and De Marco, Tom Conte and Joe Beltrami.

Which is in one sense perfectly fair – until that wave, from Barga and Piccinisco, reached our shores in the 1890s, the ordinary Scot could not afford a shop-bought meal. So perhaps we assume that those economic migrants, as they would now be labelled, were all cooks and waiters back home in one of the two small villages which produced them.

Of course, they weren't – overwhelmingly, they were peasants and labourers who spotted a niche marketing opportunity which the host population had ignored. One which required little capital, vast amounts of hard work, and the particular strengths of the family business.

I sometimes wonder what equivalent effect might a reverse migration have had. Would the Italians assume that a Scozzese ran a dram-shop, or struggled to sell oatmeal to a pasta and polenta culture?

Joe Pieri's family came from Barga, moving not only from warm and Catholic Italy to cold and Presbyterian Scotland, but also from a small village to Scotland's largest city, still in the late summer of its industrial might. In the teeth of prejudice, they established themselves within a doubly alien environment, and in an area which would have intimidated many native Scots of doucer upbringing. Indeed, this lightly-fictionalised memoir is quite as instructive about that city to the non-Glaswegian Scot as it is about the struggles of an immigrant community. Glaswegians, of course, will love it. Joe's (Mario's) Cowcaddens is a Runyonesque Hell's Kitchen, peopled with hard men, brassy whores, high-rollers and safe-crackers, uncomplicated polis and streetwise neds.

Just as we learnt to appreciate fish suppers and ultimately ciabatta, many of these immigrants took up golf and other Scottish pastimes, and nurtured and encouraged hopes for better futures for their children. It is a success story of which we should all be proud, and which should inspire those Scots who maintain that we should now close our doors.

I first met Joe when making my radio series *Scotland's Century*. It was brilliantly produced by Sharon Mair (née Arcari). It, and indeed Scotland, would have been much the poorer without the Italian Connection. *Avanti Popolo!*

Colin Bell, Balerno, August 1999.

INTRODUCTION
The Cowcaddens

*I*n the years 1920 to 1950 Glasgow was a city of stark contrasts. The city centre, heart of commercial and shopping activities, boasted some of the finest examples of Victorian and Edwardian architecture to be seen outside London. Sauchiehall Street was world-renowned for its elegant shops, and the imposing banks and offices of Renfield Street and Buchanan Street, culminating in the imposing grandeur of the City Chambers in George Square, underlined the right of Glasgow to carry the title of the 'second city of the Empire'. There was, however, another and darker side to the place. Glasgow had some of the worst slums to be found in western Europe. In the same way that Sauchiehall Street stood for elegance, the word Gorbals stood for filth and squalor and crime. There were many such slum areas on three points of the compass around the city, each of them built near industrial complexes which

1

depended on the inhabitants of the tenements for the manpower necessary for production in the labour-intensive shipbuilding yards, steel mills, factories and dockyards on which the wealth of the city was based. The west end of the city had no slums. This was the area where the wealthy lived and where they built their often palatial houses. This is true of every other British industrial city: the slum and working class districts lay north, east and south, and the well-off lived on the western side of the urban area. The prevailing wind in the British Isles is from the west, so the west end of each town and city is relatively free from the stench and pollution of industry so that those in the city's west end always enjoy fresh westerly winds (when they blow…).

One of these working class areas with its good share of noxious slum dwellings was the Cowcaddens, a district which began immediately north of Sauchiehall Street, with Renfrew Street, which ran parallel to its famous neighbour, as the line of demarcation from the city centre. The Cowcaddens was different from other Glasgow slum areas in that it lay side by side with the glamorous city centre, and the imposing Victorian and Edwardian architecture, together with the glittering expensive shops and the opulent cinema and theatre dream palaces were separated from it only by the width of a single road. For those living in the Cowcaddens to cross Renfrew Street into Sauchiehall Street was to enter another world. Left behind were the dark and forbidding tenements with their 'close' entrance, cramped back yards and overflowing middens, and to walk along Sauchiehall Street and its neighbouring Renfield Street was to see and taste a world of wealth and gracious living which was in stark contrast to their daily reality.

The traffic was not one-way, however. Many of the shop and office workers of the city centre and many cinema

and theatre-goers crossed north into Renfrew Street as customers of the variety of shops, pubs and restaurants that flourished in the area. These shops very often offered the same goods and services as did their more elegant counterparts in the city centre, and the difference in the prices charged was consolation enough for having to put up with less comfortable and opulent surroundings. Although many of the Cowcaddens pubs were no better than drinking dens, many others were as good as could be found anywhere, and names like The Atholl Arms, Jock Mills Variety Bar, The Glen Afton and Dunbar's were prominent in any discussion by the drinkers of Glasgow as to the relative merits of city public houses.

Eating places in the district were relatively few, however, and while you found one pub every two tenement blocks, restaurants – or what passed for them – were easily outnumbered by pubs, ten to one.

The working masses of the day lived no more than a penny tram ride from their place of work, and having a 'meal out' at lunch was unheard of. A 'piece', carried in a bag or lunch box to their shop or factory sufficed for the midday meal and in the evening, as like as not, the breadwinner would find on his plate a fish supper bought at the local 'Tally' fish and chip shop.

These then are a few stories, written under the guise of 'Mario', about some of the colourful characters who walked those streets, frequented the pubs and who were regular customers in one of those fish and chip shops – The Savoy.

Joe Pieri, Lenzie, August 1999

CHAPTER 1

Sadie

*S*adie was a streetwalker. Well past her sell-by date, she still plied her ancient trade regularly along the pavements of Hope Street in the knowledge that liberally applied make-up and the indifferent gas street lighting of the day were sufficient to hide her ravaged appearance from any would-be client. Not that the drunken pub-crawlers who made use of her services were discerning purchasers. She was available and she was cheap: a few shillings would buy a few fumbled moments up a close or in a back yard, and for a few coppers more the quick use of a room in one of the many shebeens in Wemyss Street was available.

Business was always very brisk for the army of streetwalkers who descended on the city centre at night. The year was 1931, the casual sex of the present day unheard of and most of those in search of the pleasures of the flesh were

forced to seek them along the pavements of the city. Sadie's beat ranged from Cowcaddens Street in the north to St Vincent Street in the south. She ventured no further down towards the river in search of customers. Although there were rich pickings in the Central Station area, at her age and with her shopworn looks, even with bad street lighting she would have been no match for the younger and infinitely far more attractive prostitutes who worked the lucrative streets in the immediate vicinity of the Central Station, where, because of the quality of the merchandise, the going rate for a few moments work was higher than anywhere else in the city.

For Sadie there was one great advantage in working the upper Hope Street beat. She was never more than a couple of minutes away from her favourite place for rest and recreation, The Savoy. Here she spent a great deal of time each hour drinking tea and resting in between clients, or did until The Savoy changed hands early in 1931, and her routine was shattered.

By the late thirties The Savoy was eventually to become something of an institution in the district. It stood at the very edge of the Cowcaddens at the corner of Hope Street and Renfrew Street, at the border of cinema and theatreland and was surrounded by a sea of public houses ranging from the posh Guy's and Lauders down through the less elaborate Atholl Arms and Glen Afton to the many drinking dens frequented by the less savoury elements of the Cowcaddens. The Savoy drew its custom from the richly variegated spectrum of humanity attracted to the area by all these amenities and it profited also by the custom provided by the inhabitants of the densely populated tenements behind it, whose staple diet, fortunately for the Petri family who had come into ownership of the place in 1931, seemed to consist largely of fish suppers, pies and chips and black puddings.

Towards the end of the thirties The Savoy had acquired a well-deserved reputation for good inexpensive food and did a brisk trade from early morning breakfasts until midnight, the closing time of the carry-out section. The nature of the clientele changed according to the time of day. The Garnethill area immediately to the northwest was well supplied with lodging houses very popular with the artistes appearing at nearby theatres, and many of them would breakfast at The Savoy on the way to rehearsals. From midday onwards lunches and light snacks were served, very popular with shoppers in Sauchiehall Street. Next would come the teatime trade, when theatre and cinema goers would partake of The Savoy's famous fish teas prior to a visit to their chosen place of entertainment. After teatime The Savoy would change character quite radically. Off would come the tablecloths, revealing the plain marble tops of the tables, away would come the pretty cruet sets, to be replaced by plain glass vinegar and sauce bottles and metal salt dishes, the menu cards were replaced by a menu board hung on the wall with no more than half a dozen items on it, the good quality crockery and cutlery in use until then was put away and well worn chipped and cracked substitutes laid out in their place.

The stage was now set for the culmination of the day's trade – the pub rush. In those days all bars were made to close at 10pm, at which time a tide of humanity in various stages of inebriation, all now in search of food to quell the pangs of their alcohol-induced hunger spilled onto the pavements. To prevent the entry of the worst drunks The Savoy boasted of a chucker-out (*see chapter 9*), but even so after 10pm the restaurant was packed with a seething mass of semi-drunks whose table manners and general behaviour made the change of table set-up necessary if expensive breakages and pilfering were to be avoided.

The Savoy had often considered closing early to avoid the stressful hours between 10pm and midnight, but the truth of the matter was that almost as much business was done during the hectic pub rush as had been done during the previous 10 hours. Moreover, these late night customers were not in a state to be discerning, so any food not deemed fit for the genteel day trade was served up to them, thereby swelling the profits of the establishment.

The development of The Savoy into what was undoubtedly one of the best fish and chip shops in Glasgow had not been an easy task however. In 1931 it was no better than many of the drinking dens in the district, and because of the rough nature of its clientele a very strong arm was needed to run it. Such an arm was possessed in abundance by Francesco Petri, head of the family who came into the ownership of the little fish and chip shop in that year. He was then 53 years of age, no more than five feet five inches tall, but he was thickset and possessed of the strength of a bull. His life had been hard. Born of a poor peasant family in a Tuscan hamlet, he emigrated to the USA in his early teens to find work, as did millions of his fellow countrymen. Possessing no special skills he worked in a variety of jobs until recalled to Italy for military service in 1914. He survived three years of war against Austria in the northern Italian Alps. Despite the glowing promises of the politicians, conditions in Italy were as bad as ever after the war, if not worse, and in order to provide for himself and his family, for he was now married with two sons, he had once more to seek work abroad. The United States Government had by now set up a quota system of immigration under which people of Mediterranean origin were barred from free entry into the country, so where could he go?

The local priest spoke of a place called Glasgow in the country of Scotland far to the north, where Italian families had

7

emigrated and where work was to be found, and where he had church connections who could help find lodgings and work. With their few belongings packed, the Petri family set out, and arrived in Glasgow four days later, for that was the time it took in those days for such a journey.

Francesco worked hard, saved what money he could, and finally at the beginning of the thirties found himself the proud owner of a little fish and chip shop, The Savoy. This shop had had several owners in its 10 years' existence, but none of them had lasted long. The place was just too difficult to run. Set at the edge of the city centre it was flanked at the rear by pubs and drinking dens, and the street corner on which it stood served as bus terminal for the mining towns on the outskirts of Glasgow. The area was a stamping ground for the hordes of prostitutes who worked the streets in the vicinity, and at night The Savoy was a focal point for this low life. It did a roaring trade, but drunks, prostitutes and toughs abounded and fights and disturbances were nightly occurrences. Small wonder then that the shop had changed hands so many times in so few years; each owner put up with the dreadful place for a short time for the sake of the money to be made, but then moved on, nerves frayed and courage exhausted. Francesco, however, was made of sterner stuff.

He could see the potential of the place if a better class of customer could be attracted, so he began the slow process of weeding out the riff-raff and of making The Savoy a place which decent people could frequent.

In this he was helped by three things. First, his physical strength and courage. He was more than capable of dealing with the toughs and drunks who came about the place; there was never a fight started nor a disturbance created that Francesco could not handle. Second, a proper bus terminal was built some distance from the shop, siphoning

the drunken miners and most of the prostitutes away from the immediate area, and the third very important factor was police sergeant 'Black' Alec McCrae. Black Alec was an old friend of Francesco; during the war several Scottish regiments had been sent to the northern Italian Front to help stem the Austrian advance after the debacle at Caporetto, and there the two had met, fighting side by side in the bitter battles on the Piave and forging a friendship which was to be continued in later years. For to Francesco's delight, on taking over his new shop, he discovered that his wartime companion was now a sergeant in the police, and patrolled The Savoy district. Black Alec, too, was happy to renew the friendship.

'That's a bloody rough place you've landed yourself with, Frank, but if you want to sort it out, I'll back you up. The first thing you've got to do is bar all the brass nails – those whores bring nothing but trouble. Then clean out the neds and riff-raff. Don't kill anybody, but hit 'em hard and I'll run 'em in.' And so the place was cleaned up. The whores were told in no uncertain terms to go elsewhere and take their customers with them, and the toughs and troublemakers were given short shrift. If necessary they felt the heavy weight of Frank's fists, then were subjected to a much more merciless hammering by Black Alec and his squad before spending a night in the cells. In a very short time The Savoy was transformed; word quickly spread amongst the troglodytes of the district; don't go near that place – you'll get a tanking if you do. At first business suffered; instead of an unruly mass of drunks and low life, at night very few tables were occupied, but as word of the relative tranquillity to be found there spread, new customers were attracted, and soon the same volume of business as before was being done. There were lots of drunken customers of course; there were very few walking the streets at night then who were not frequenters of pubs, but

9

not the dregs of humanity to be found there six months before.

And so, together with scores of others Sadie was barred from the comfort of her operational headquarters of long standing. She did not take kindly to this and persisted in returning time after time to her old haunt, always with a customer on her arm, and would shriek abuse on Frank's head on being escorted firmly to the door, imploring the help of her client for the night, who invariably would take one look at Frank's massive forearms and stony glare and always decide that his fair lady was not worth risking injury for.

But one night Sadie managed to sneak in quickly without being noticed, accompanied not merely by one, but by three clients, and by the time Frank had become aware of her presence she had seated herself down at an empty wall table in a small side room which at the time was free of other customers. These tables were heavy marble affairs with iron legs bolted into a terrazzo floor, and Sadie had lodged herself between the table and the wall to await events. They were not long in coming. Francesco looked up, saw her vanish into the side room with her three customers, sighed, came from behind the counter wiping his hands on his apron and stood before her.

'Come on Sadie, out you get, you know you're barred from here.'

Sadie answered with a barrage of invective at the man who had deprived her of her favourite haunt and gave notice of her refusal to move. Frank let her finish, taking the time to size up her companions, saw that they were smallish, weedy and drunk and discounted them immediately as constituting no physical threat in the event of trouble. Always a man of few words, he went into action. He grabbed hold of Sadie's left wrist and pulled hard. She always walked and sat with her left

arm crossed over her ample bosom, and she was sitting thus, but with her other hand holding on tightly to the iron table leg. Frank pulled hard again but could not budge the heavy body wedged between wall and table. He took a deep breath and pulled again, this time with all his strength. There was a sudden sharp cracking noise of splintering buckles, leather straps and wire stays as Sadie's false arm was torn from her body. There followed a second's motionless silence. Francesco stood open-mouthed, staring incredulously at the remnants of Sadie's arm clutched in his fist. Her three companions sat frozen and Sadie kept holding on to the table with her good arm. Suddenly the place erupted. Sadie screamed, and promptly fainted; her three clients moved to stand up and Frank, sensing their motion but not waiting to see what their intentions were, set about them with three mighty blows from what now remained of Sadie's arm, knocking them stiff to the floor, unconscious.

As chance would have it two of Black Alec's men were in the back shop drinking coffee and were promptly summoned. Sadie's three clients, now conscious, pleaded innocence to all wrong doing, which was of course true, and were sent sternly on their way. Sadie, now tearful and minus an arm, vowed never to set foot in The Savoy again, and was escorted home by the policemen, where she was helped to fit on another arm, of which she carried a stock of two. She was seen often in The Savoy in later years, where, having given up her old line of work and having opted for respectability, she would partake daintily and one-handedly of a fish tea before going to the pictures or theatre once a week.

Frank had long retired, but she always paused for a word with his son Mario, who had witnessed the incident and who now ran the family business.

'Hello, Mario, how's yir faither? Day ye remember the

night he pullt the arm affa me? Aye, he wuz a great man yir faither wuz.'

Sadie's weekly visits to The Savoy continued until 1971, by which time she was well into her old age and could walk only with the aid of a walking stick. Then, for the second time in 40 years she was deprived of her favourite haunt. The Savoy was demolished to make way for the redevelopment of the Cowcaddens, and on its corner site there now stands an imposing modern structure, the Royal Scottish Academy of Music and Drama.

In the first 10 years of its life The Savoy had five owners. For the next 40 years it remained in the hands of one family.

CHAPTER 2

Sandy MacKenzie

*A*t the peak of his powers some 15 years back in the early twenties Sandy McKenzie had been a superb figure of a man. Born in the little mining village of Cumnock just after the turn of the century, he had inherited the strength and stamina of his miner father, and the spartan environment of Scottish country life in those days had helped to shape and temper his natural endowment of physical power and strength.

During World War I, lured by the prospect of better wages in the big city, the McKenzie family moved to Glasgow and found lodgings in a grimy soot-stained tenement in the Cowcaddens, barely a stone's throw away from the glamorous and legendary Sauchiehall Street. There, at the age of 14, his rudimentary schooling now over, the young Sandy, big and powerful for his years, readily found employment as a coalman in the Buchanan Street station goods yard, working

nine hours a day shovelling coal from goods trains into hundredweight sacks and loading them on to horse drawn carts for delivery to factories and households in the Glasgow area.

These were the days when boxing booths were a feature of the many travelling fun fairs, 'Shows' as they were called by the locals, which served as cheap entertainment for the working classes. If you were willing and able to absorb physical punishment in the boxing ring by standing up to the resident pugilist, your weekly wage of two pounds ten shillings or so could be augmented by as much as a pound by the simple process of standing up to a battering for a period of five minutes without being knocked down.

These so-called pugilists were little better than professional thugs, skilled in every dirty trick of the boxing ring, and the contenders who could stand up to a barrage of low blows, kidney and rabbit punches and the occasional eye gouging for even half of the prescribed five minutes were very few and far between.

But the hard-muscled young Sandy could give as much as he received, and could be sure of winning a pocketful of beer money every time one of these Shows came to the neighbourhood. As time went on the young coalman became heavier, stronger and as well versed in the art of physical mayhem as were the beer-bellied toughs who served as resident boxers in the tawdry booths. He began to frequent the many boxing gyms which flourished near the city centre, and there, in a Sauchiehall Street gym run by the British champion Johnny McMillan, he caught the notice of one Ted McGowan, a boxing manager and fight promoter well known in Glasgow circles.

Impressed by the strength and boxing craft of the young Sandy, McGowan soon had him under his wing, and

every other week the tough young coalman would be matched with fighters in proper ring conditions until he gained the dizzy title of light-heavyweight champion of the whole of Scotland. In the process, however, he absorbed a tremendous amount of physical punishment. His cauliflower ears and thickened nose bore witness to the many punches he had absorbed in the process of earning the few pounds which served as prize money in those far-off days of boxing. The apotheosis of his career came in 1932, when for the princely sum of £300, for after all, this was as much as a man could earn in two years' work, he was mismatched with the American Tommy Loughran, one of the most skilful boxers in the history of the ring, and who was on his way to becoming light-heavyweight champion of the world.

The fight lasted for seven rounds, the knockout in the last round signalling the end of Sandy's career as a boxer, for in the one-sided contest he took so much punishment that he was unable ever to box again. And now in 1935 he was a shambling punch-drunk shadow of his powerful former self. He had no job, and augmented his few shillings 'Broo' money by filling and delivering the odd bag of coal from the Buchanan Street coal depot. He had never married, and lived alone in a room and kitchen in a dank tenement in the Cowcaddens. His way of life was monotonous and simple. A walk to the coal yard in the morning, in the hope of finding some odd job to do, then on to the bookie's for a shilling bet on the horses, then on to the pub where there was always someone ready to stand him a pint for the sake of the good old successful days. Unsteadily, then, for the tiniest amount of alcohol seemed to have an immediate effect on his punch-damaged nervous system, he would stagger on to The Savoy for his main meal of the day, a nightly fish supper. In The Savoy he always sat where he could see out from the window, dull

eyes following the movement of pedestrians on the pavement and the mixture of horse drawn carts and motor cars in the street beyond. He ate slowly and methodically with his fingers, disdaining the use of knife and fork, alternately blowing his nose and wiping greasy fingers on a soot-stained handkerchief. Napkins were only for the posh restaurants; a shilling fish supper hardly warranted one.

The Savoy was not only ideally situated for theatre and cinema-goers, but also for constables on the beat out of the northern police station, which lay 100 yards away. At The Savoy they could meet to exchange notes and refresh themselves with tea, or something stronger for those so minded. Moreover, next to the Hope Street entrance to The Savoy stood a police box, and those on duty would call in to the station from time to time, so where better to spend an illicit half hour than next door in the back shop of The Savoy. It was well known that The Savoy was hardly ever without the presence of a constable, and if any of the local public wanted a policeman for some reason, the 'Tally's' was the place.

As Sandy McKenzie sat eating his haddock and chips, there was as usual, a policeman on the premises, enjoying the last few puffs of a cigarette before going out to look for his mate on the beat. John McArthur was young and had only been a few months on the force. His partner was a much more experienced constable who had as yet not appeared for duty and as John stood brushing the cigarette ash from his uniform, he heard urgent shouts coming from the front shop.

'Polis! Polis! Help! Polis! There's murder out here!'

The young rookie rushed out to the front door of the restaurant and stopped dead in his tracks. On the far pavement of Renfrew Street at The Savoy Cinema ticket booth, stood a huge man in sailor's uniform. As he swayed from side-to-side, unintelligible shouts came from his distorted mouth. In his

hand he held a murderous-looking carving knife with which he slashed wildly at the air. The crowd waiting to enter the cinema had scattered away from the menace of the slicing blade. No one seemed to have been wounded, but the girl in the ticket booth was screaming hysterically, and panic was spreading in the tightly-packed crowd as people tried to escape the threat of the lunging knife.

John McArthur took a deep breath to steady himself, unsheathed his truncheon and stepped across to confront the crazed sailor.

'Drop the knife!'

He yelled in the strongest voice he could muster, but the sailor paid no heed. Instead, with a target identified, he began to advance towards the hesitant young policeman, the knife in his hand making evil little flicking motions in the air. Sandy McKenzie's enjoyment of his fish supper had been rudely interrupted by the shouting and commotion in the street. With crumbs of food stuck to his lips, he stood up, and went to the door of the shop as the young policeman and the sailor advanced towards one another, the one with a truncheon and the other with a wicked-looking knife in his hand. Sandy sized up the situation and moved up beside the policeman. He pushed the young rookie aside, and stepped up to confront the advancing sailor. The years seemed to miraculously lift from his shoulders, a brightness replaced the dullness in the eyes, and the shuffling gait became a light springy step. He dropped into a boxer's stance, left arm with clenched fist extended, right fist across his chest, weaving and crouching in front of the armed man. The latter paused for a moment then made a vicious lunge at him with the knife. Sandy timed his move to perfection, he ducked under the slashing blade, and hit the man with a hooking left-handed punch to the solar plexus, delivered with all the resurrected

power in Sandy's body. Gasping like a stranded fish for breath, the sailor dropped his knife, and was finished off by a pounding right-handed blow to the side of his face.

A relieved John McArthur secured the unconscious man's hands with a pair of handcuffs and turned to Sandy, profuse in his thanks .

'Thass awright' was the answer, 'couldnay havum cuttin up the polis' and Sandy returned to his fish supper.

CHAPTER 3

The Bookie's Runner

The bookie's runner is now an extinct species. The legalisation of the betting shop some years ago sounded the death knell of the street bookie, and with them there vanished from the streets of Glasgow their runners, whose function it was to act as minder, bet collector and look-out for their bookie employers.

In those far-off days when each High Street did not boast its quota of plush and well-appointed betting shops as it does now, the average working class punter who wanted a shilling flutter on the dogs and horses had to rely on the services of the illegal street bookie. Cash betting, except on the actual racecourse, was illegal, and the vast majority of the betting population were not creditworthy enough to indulge in the luxury of a postal or phone bet with the accredited firms of bookies, who went by the grandiose title of 'Turf Accountants'. Nor was it in the main possible for them to visit

19

the racecourse to place a bet. Therefore the illegal street bookie flourished.

Not only was it illegal for these street bookies to operate, but it was also against the law for any citizen to make cash bets with them, and in the course of time a well-defined system for the evasion of these laws was developed. Each bookie had his own area of operation or 'pitch', which was jealously guarded against interlopers, who took the form either of rival gangs or of the police, The police periodically raided the illicit premises, usually a house, in order to enforce the law. At the centre of the operation was the bookie himself, (or herself, for one of the best-known bookies in the Cowcaddens area was the famous 'Ma Bell') surrounded and protected by his various 'runners'. These runners were graded in a well-defined hierarchy, the more intelligent and trustworthy being given the job of accepting the shillings and half-crowns from the punters, and the ones with more brawn than brain, the so-called 'hard men', had the job of protecting the pitch from any marauding invader. The dangers that beset these runners were many and varied. Scroungers abounded, as did violent thieves who would assault them for the gain of a few shillings, and they had to deal regularly with the hard-luck tales of punters who did not have ready cash to pay their dues. The hooks, crooks and comic singers who hung around the bookies' pitch were many and varied, and it was the runner's job to deal with them all.

It was also their job to be on the alert for any approaching members of the police, for the pitches were the constant targets for police raids, and whenever the 'polis' were spotted, the cry of 'Edge Up' would be heard, alerting the head-bookie that a raid was imminent. In general, however, the police looked upon the street bookies with a great deal of indulgence, and a tacit modus vivendi had grown up between

them over the years. Indeed, news of impending raids would often be leaked to the bookies, who would clear their pitch of clients, for it would never do to have the customers arrested. In their place the police would find the odd dozen or so denizens of the local dosshouse, who were herded into the waiting Black Marias, put into overnight cells and then hauled in front of the local magistrate, who would compliment the police on their zeal and fine the offenders 10 shillings or so each. The fine would be immediately paid by one of the trusted runners, and the happy convicted men would be given a few shillings for their trouble and treated to a fish supper at the local Tally's as a further reward.

The Cowcaddens area was well supplied with bookies, the area having a dozen or so pitches, all of them named after the owner of the operation. There was Joe Docherty's pitch in Wemyss Street, just off Hope Street behind The Savoy Restaurant; there was Ma Bell's in Cowcaddens Street, Alec Campbell's at the Round Toll, and John Foy's at the top of West Nile Street where cart horses used to drag heavy loads up the incline to the Buchanan Street goods station. This latter did not number many 'hard men' amongst his runners, for he himself was the hardest of the hard, his scarred face bearing witness to the numerous razor fights of his younger days as a runner in the tough Garngad area and his fearsome reputation was enough to discourage any hooks and crooks away from his pitch. There was also the legendary Laurie Ventre from the Garscube Road, of Italian descent, who over the years had acquired a Robin Hood-like reputation because of his generosity to the denizens of that neighbourhood. His death in the sixties was mourned in the Garscube Road by a funeral to rival that of any Chicago godfather, with carloads of flowers and hundreds of mourners who afterwards set new records for the amount of liquor consumed in the local pubs. The local

constabulary was much in evidence too, not only to pay their respects to an esteemed and valued adversary but also to keep the peace in the event of friction between the opposing factions present at the funeral.

The most lucrative and best known pitch in the Cowcaddens was that of Joe Docherty. It was a large family run business, reigned over by the polished and always impeccably dressed Joe with the help of two sisters, Sadie and Patsy. A brother, Sam, had for a while been involved but his somewhat shady dealings and doubtful connections had forced Joe to distance himself from his brother's questionable activities. These activities had culminated in the much publicised Bank Of Scotland case of the early sixties. One Monday morning two of Sam's runners (he had at that time set up a pitch of his own) presented themselves at the Cowcaddens Street branch of the bank with a sum of money to be deposited in Sam's account. One of them wrote out a deposit slip, the teller checked the cash and gave the runner a receipted counterfoil for the amount deposited. That amount was £8,000, a very large sum for those days, but what the teller had failed to notice was that the figure on the deposit slip had inadvertently been set down as £80,000, a mistake of one zero digit.

Sam was not slow in noticing this, and when his monthly statement came in from the bank, he decided to chance his arm and proceeded to ask indignantly as to why his statement was £72,000 short, and produced his receipt as proof of the bank's mistake. The bank quite properly contested that the affair was simply a teller's error in misreading the sum written on the deposit slip, and that no such massive sum as £80,000 had ever been deposited. So with the help of a lawyer whose name shall not be recorded here, Sam took the bank to court in an attempt to have the bank honour its receipt. A succession of hooks, crooks and comic singers recruited from

Sam's Cowcaddens connections queued up to testify on Sam's behalf, swearing that in fact £80,000 had been put into the bank on that day.

The case, which became a cause célèbre of the day, was heard by a sceptical Sheriff Carmont, later to become the famous Lord Carmont. He duly listened to the evidence, and when it became plain that such a sum, in five pound notes as claimed by the motley parade of witnesses, would have required several large trunks for storage, threw the case out of court, making it plain to the unashamed Sam that he was lucky to escape a charge of attempted fraud. The affair did not endear Joe to his brother, for he believed in the principle that if you were a fly man you had to be an honest fly man, and not an obvious rascal.

However, to return to the main theme. Situated but a stone's throw from Sauchiehall Street, close to the Pavilion and Royal Theatres and surrounded by dozens of pubs, Joe Docherty's was a very busy pitch indeed and a potential dripping roast for predators. Therefore he had to surround himself with reliable runners, with emphasis on the hard men and only the best would be picked to work for Joe Docherty. Possibly the best of these best was a certain Johnny Myres. You might be justified in thinking that the young Johnny had been specially genetically bred for the job of hard man. Short and squat in build he had the physique and strength of an ox. A bullet head sat squarely on massive shoulders with no visible neckline, and powerful arms terminated in thick fingers that could form themselves into rock hard intimidating fists when clenched. Nature, however, had been less generous in the allocation of brain cells, and his fearsome physical attributes were by no means matched by his intellectual powers, which were exactly in inverse proportion to his brawn. But he was perfect for the part of hard man bookie's runner; give him an

23

order, zip up the back of his head, and Johnny could be relied on to carry out his duties to the letter. If he was on your side, you always felt safe with Johnny around.

In common with many of the young of the day, (or of any day for that matter) Johnny enjoyed a refreshment, which is another way of saying that he could partake copiously of strong drink, and whilst the amount he occasionally consumed would have felled a lesser man, the only sign that Johnny had been drinking was an increase in his natural truculence. Never given to witty conversation, after a few whiskies he would become even less communicative than usual, more easily irritated, and wise men knew that at these times it was best to leave Johnny strictly alone. Despite his occupation and disposition only once had he been in trouble with the police, and that because of an unfortunate misunderstanding.

Hogmanay in those days in Glasgow was a time when all redblooded men got roaring drunk for two or three consecutive days to celebrate the New Year, and first-footers would stagger from house to house in a perpetual whisky haze, exchanging drinks both with friends and perfect strangers in a maudlin profession of goodwill for the New Year. Goodwill that is, until the question of religious affiliation came up, or the subject of football, which also had religious connotations, as demonstrated in the two Glasgow teams, Celtic and Rangers, and if the stranger you were drinking with happened to be of a different persuasion, goodwill would vanish, and many a beer bottle would be broken over many an opposing head.

This particular Hogmanay had gone well with Johnny. For two days beer, whisky and cheap wine had flowed liberally, with never a cross word to disturb the New Year festivities, and now after two days without sleep and sodden

with drink, even his exceptional physique felt the need for rest. Tiredness came over him whilst drinking in a stranger's house, and seeing a bed in the corner of the room he collapsed into it and fell immediately into a drunken sleep. Unknown to him, also in the bed was the lady of the house, who also had collapsed in an alcoholic stupor some time previously and the two of them lay there, oblivious to one another's presence. Now, when two people of the opposite sex are sharing the same bed it is quite logical for the husband of one to assume that they are not there for the purpose of saying their prayers, and the next morning, when the husband of the lady in question returned home to find a complete stranger in bed with his wife he jumped to the natural conclusion.

Enraged, he picked up a handy hammer and began setting about the sleeping man with it, but the badly-aimed blows were fortunately largely absorbed by a combination of heavy bed clothes and Johnny's bulk. They served only to awaken him rudely, and finding himself the object of a completely unprovoked attack, he defended himself vigorously. In no time at all the indignant Johnny had turned the tables on his assailant and the unfortunate husband found himself at the receiving end of Johnny's fists.

The poor man was saved from grievous harm only by the fact that Johnny was still well befuddled with drink and thus not too precise with his blows and the screams of his wife, who awoke from her drunken sleep to see her husband being set about by a complete stranger. It took the efforts of three large policemen to arrest Johnny and drag him to the Maitland Police Station cells. Next morning, still protesting his innocence, he was hauled in front of the magistrate and fined one pound for a breach of the peace. This one brush with the law had left a brooding sense of the injustice of life in Johnny's psyche.

A regular meeting place for Joe Docherty and his

runners was The Savoy, just a few yards round from the pitch in Wemyss Street, an arrangement which suited the owner Mario down to the ground, for not only was it good business for him, but also the occasional presence of these local hard men was a disincentive to possible visits from unwelcome marauding toughs who plagued pub and restaurant owners with demands for money. Johnny Myres ate all his meals there, and although occasionally he would forget to pay, these lapses were always overlooked by Mario, who looked upon them as well placed insurance premiums.

One night late, after the dog tracks had closed and the day's business finished, Johnny was standing at the counter of The Savoy, devouring a fish supper from a paper wrapping, as was his habit. Customers were not allowed to stand at the counter to eat in such a fashion, but Mario always thought it politic never to remonstrate with the volatile Johnny; he was a fast eater and did not linger long. Mario stood and watched him shovel up pieces of fish with his not too clean hands, and as he did so, out of the corner of his eye he noticed a flurry of movement at one of the tables in the restaurant, as two tough looking individuals started to make their way out of the shop. One of them had a shiny object in his hand, and as he passed behind the unsuspecting Johnny, hit him a blow to the back of the head. The runner spat out a mouthful of half-chewed food, turned as quick as a flash and smashed a clenched fist into his attacker's face, knocking him to the ground. Then with a bellow of pain and rage he turned to the second of the toughs, who had started to run towards the door, and kicked him as hard as he could in the back. The man bounced hard against the wall and collapsed in an unconscious heap.

Johnny turned to the thunderstruck Mario.

'Whut did he dae tay the back o' ma heid?' and turned the back of his head for inspection. Mario's jaw dropped in

amazement, for there, imbedded in the base of Johnny's skull was a table knife, the tip of its blade well buried into the bone.

'Pull the fuckin' thing oot!'

Mario did as instructed, and had to exert a fair deal of strength to release the knife, which had penetrated about a full quarter inch into the skull.

The police were summoned and the two men were identified by Johnny as hooligans who had tried to pay off an old score. Joe confirmed that the runner was blameless in the matter, so the two, bleeding profusely and still semi-conscious, were promptly bundled off under arrest. Johnny refused to go for medical attention, and after the wound had been washed and disinfected by a still incredulous Mario, went home to sleep it all off. The next day he appeared at the pitch as usual, none the worse for wear, complaining only of a stiff neck and a bit of a sore head.

About 35 years after these events this story had a sequel. Mario was by this time retired and living part of the year on the island of Majorca. One night, as he and his wife Mary were leaving the entrance of a plush hotel after having enjoyed a meal and a cabaret there, a large black Mercedes limousine drew up and disgorged four passengers: two youths and two heavily painted Spanish-looking women. The two young men spoke with a distinct Glasgow accent Mario noticed, as he and Mary paused to let them pass. The front door of the limo opened, and from the seat next to the driver there emerged slowly the squat, bulky figure of a man. Features could not be made out in the dim light, but the shape with its bull neck seemed oddly familiar, and as the man came into the brighter light of the foyer recognition was complete.

'My God, it's Johnny Myers!'

It was indeed, older and greyer of course, but still rock solid and as powerful as ever. The squat figure turned.

27

'Jesus! It's Mario!'

and Mario was almost knocked out by an affectionate pat on the back, was caught up in bear hug and left with feet dangling off the ground as Johnny expressed his delight in seeing his old friend again after all those years.

'Hi, Mario, dae ye remember the night those bastards stuck a knife in ma heid ? Aye, we hud sum great times in they days! Ah'm here tae look aifter these two boys fur a pal a mine back in Glasgow.'

Introductions were made as Johnny kept pounding Mario on the back.

'You tell'um Mario. You tell'um aboot the auld days in The Savoy. You tell'um aboot the night they bastards stuck a knife in ma heid.'

And so Mario told the story and advised the two youths, 'You're a couple of lucky fellas having Johnny look after you. He's the best in the business.'

CHAPTER 4

Fabio

abio was a regular customer of The Savoy. He enjoyed a fish tea there two or three times a week, was well liked by the waitresses, for he was a lavish tipper, and always had a cheery word to say to Mario, the owner, who invariably responded in kind (as he did to all his customers, at least to those who did not have to be ejected from time-to-time by Big Steve the chucker-out). There was nothing remarkable about being a regular customer at The Savoy: there were many such, given the excellence of the fare, and people came regularly from far and wide to eat what Mario proudly claimed to be the best fish and chips to be had in Glasgow .

The remarkable thing about Fabio however, was the fact that he himself owned a fish and chip shop in the east end of the city, and it was rather unusual for the owner of a business to be such a regular patron of a similar type of

29

establishment, unless, and the suspicion had once crossed Mario's mind, the visits had the ulterior motive of monitoring cooking methods or of poaching staff. But as time passed it became obvious that such suspicions were unfounded, and when Fabio's real occupation finally was revealed to Mario, all doubts were laid to rest.

The truth of the matter was that although Fabio did indeed own a small fish and chip shop in the London Road area, he himself took very little part in the running of it. He had, if one may use the pun, other fish to fry. His occupation was not listed in any trades or professional directory, indeed, to describe his activities a word will have to be coined. He was in fact a cash courier, a term which has to be explained.

In those far off days of the fifties rigid currency controls were in effect, which meant that only companies and individuals engaged in importing and exporting business activities were able to engage in monetary transactions outwith the United Kingdom. Any private individual travelling to Europe, or anywhere else for that matter, on private business or on holiday, was limited to taking with him the munificent sum of £40 each year, an amount which would just suffice for the traveller to pay for the odd cup of coffee and the occasional gin and tonic when anywhere abroad, even at the very low prices of those days. It is a sad fact of life that whenever any government passes any such draconian laws, there are always to be found individuals who will try to satisfy the market and will seek to find ways around such regulations. A lively black market will flourish under such circumstances, patronised only too willingly by a populace that finds constrictions of such a nature stifling and unjust.

And so the service offered by Fabio was invented and flourished. In circumstances where no written contract was possible and where therefore the element of personal trust

was all important, Fabio travelled the length and breadth of the area now known as Strathclyde, collecting sums of money from various individuals. The amount collected from each person was meticulously entered into a little cashbook. The money collected had to be in five-pound notes, and no sum less than £200 would be accepted. This may not sound much in today's values, but it represented at least 10 times as much in today's currency. Each subscriber would give Fabio the name of a town in Europe where he wished the cash to reappear, and having parted with the money, which in some cases amounted to tens of hundreds per person, the owner of the cash would nervously await developments, for if Fabio had ever elected to abscond with his collection of five-pound notes no official redress would have been possible to the subscriber.

There was however not the slightest cause for worry; over the years Fabio had acquired the reputation of strict and meticulous honesty in his business. Some time would pass, the period depending on how quickly Fabio could collect the sum of £25,000 in such a fashion. When finally Fabio had gathered this amount, exactly £25,000, no more and no less, the money would be tidily packed into a medium-sized suitcase, and Fabio would book an overnight sleeper on the night-train to London. Once there, the contents of the suitcase would be entrusted to an individual at an address in the city, together with a list of names, amounts and towns. Fabio would then return to Glasgow the next day, always to visit The Savoy for his favourite fish tea and await events. Some time would pass, one or two weeks, sometimes more, and then on receipt of a phone call from London, Fabio would pay a quick call to each of his subscribers to inform them that a bank book awaited them in their named town. The amount in the account was in the local currency and always for the amount given originally in Scotland, less 15 per cent. A substantial part of this

deduction stayed with Fabio, the remainder having been taken off during the transfer process. Everyone was happy, the currency regulations evader took no risk of discovery by the authorities, and the commission of 15 per cent was a small price to pay in the circumstances.

Although the maximum secrecy was observed in these transactions, Fabio was only too well aware of the regular pattern of movement created by his activities. The possession of such large amounts of cash and the regularity of his train journeys to London occasioned him a certain amount of concern. He worried about the possibility of attracting the attention of criminal elements who would have been only too pleased to separate him from the contents of his suitcase and his night sleeper trips on the London train were anything but restful. He would sit awake and alert all night, tense and nervous, able to relax only when the suitcase had been delivered to the London address with the possibility of being robbed, on that trip at least, now behind him. The possibility of taking on a partner in the affair to share the burden and minimise the chance of an attack had briefly been considered but discarded. Profits would have to be shared, the chances of maintaining secrecy would be lessened, and his clients might not take kindly to having their secrets divulged to a third party.

The only other possible means of travel was either by bus or by private car, and in those pre-motorway days such a journey would have been too long and far too tiring. Suddenly however a new method of travel became possible, the aeroplane. In the middle fifties a daily air service between Renfrew Airport in Glasgow and Croydon Airport in London was inaugurated, and Fabio immediately began to make use of the new facility. Behind him now were the noisy and dirty steam railway journeys from Glasgow Central to London Euston and gone was the ever-present fear of being mugged

and robbed in the dimly lit confines of the train's night sleeper compartment. The trip by air took only two hours; the planes used were four-engine propeller-driven Vickers Viscounts and were solid and comfortable. His suitcase was of a size which could be carried as hand luggage and so the trips to London became much more pleasant, faster (the round trip could now be done in one day) and much less worrisome.

This happy state of affairs continued for some time, with Fabio waxing affluent on his share of the deducted 15 per cent, until suddenly one autumn day the pattern was shattered. The morning flight had been uneventful and Fabio was able to enjoy the view from his window seat, taking pleasure in the autumn tints of the countryside far down below, its colours softened by the misty morning sunshine of an early November dawn. The plane landed at Croydon on time, Fabio hailed a taxi and was soon at his London rendezvous.

A lift deposited Fabio on one of the upper floors of a large and affluent looking office block in the Lombard Street area, where he waited for a response to his ring at an office door. This was opened by the usual receptionist and one look at her tear stained face was enough to alert Fabio that bad news awaited. His contact had just suffered a massive heart attack and had died on the way to hospital.

What to do with his suitcase and its precious contents? Fabio had no other address to go to and no local telephone number to ring, for no such contingency had ever been envisaged. The best course of action, he reasoned, was to return to Glasgow with his merchandise, there to await instructions from the European end of the connection.

The late afternoon flight to Glasgow was almost full. Fabio sat pensively in his comfortable seat, with the powerful throb of the engines as background to the mood of sadness

and shock caused by the suddenness of the death of his business colleague. The sound of the engines had almost lulled him to sleep when his reverie was broken by the sound of an announcement.

'Good evening ladies and gentlemen, we are now approaching Renfrew Airport, but our landing will be delayed for a short while because of heavy fog which has suddenly blanketed out the Glasgow area. This is quite normal at this time of the year, the fog should clear soon and we should be landing with only about 15 minutes delay. I do hope you have enjoyed your flight.'

A hum of conversation broke out at the announcement, but as the promised 15 minutes passed and stretched out to half an hour with no sign of the plane making an attempt to land a slight unease began to spread through the passengers. This was manifest in the shuffling of feet, a glancing at wristwatches, a craning of necks to attempt a view from the darkening windows, the nervous adjusting of seatbelts and the occasional forced giggle of laughter. A second announcement came.

'Well, ladies and gentlemen, it seems that the fog is not going to lift after all. However, there is no problem, we have been diverted to Prestwick, which as you know is always fog-free. We will be landing there in a few minutes and you will be taken back to Glasgow by bus. We deeply regret the inconvenience, but I am afraid we have no control over this November weather. Thank you very much for your patience.'

The plane banked steeply and began the 25-mile descent towards Prestwick. The fog seemed to clear suddenly and the brown fields below became clearly visible in the failing light. The earth was no more than a few hundred feet under the aircraft when one of the engines began to splutter and cough, to be followed by a roughness in another, there

was a rumble of descending undercarriage and a sharp announcement over the loudspeakers.

'We are running out of fuel and will have to make an emergency landing. There is no cause for alarm however. Fasten your seatbelts and please relax.'

There was no time for the passengers to react in fright to this information, there was a sudden juddering bump, a sensation of being thrown forward by a giant hand, and then a silence as the plane came to a halt in the middle of a large flat field, its undercarriage twisted and broken by the force of the impact. There was a moment of shocked silence in the plane. The incident was over and done with so quickly that the passengers had had no time to take fright at their predicament and their only emotion was one of relief at the fact that they were now safe and unhurt on solid ground. A reassuring voice came through the loudspeakers.

'Ladies and gentlemen, there is absolutely no cause for alarm. Because of shortage of fuel we have had to make a forced landing in a field. The town of Largs is only about two miles away so help will be here in no time at all. The crew will now come round to see that everyone is all right. The undercarriage has collapsed, so the doors of the plane are at ground level. The doors will be opened, and those of you who care to stretch their legs can go outside. I thank you for your splendid behaviour in this unfortunate incident.'

The Vickers Vicount had made a miraculous landing on a field at the top of the Haylie Brae.

Fabio sat for a moment trembling with shock. A babble of animated conversation erupted amongst the passengers, a wave of joyous relief spreading through them. No one seemed to be injured by the impact: the doors of the plane were opened and a few passengers jumped out to the ground a few feet below to breathe deeply of the sharp

evening air and to examine their surroundings. His composure recovered, Fabio decided to join them, and clutching his precious case stepped out of the door. His foot caught on the sill, he stumbled and fell flat on his face on the wet grass a foot or so below. The suitcase flew out of his hand, rose into the air, then burst open on hitting the ground. A shower of banknotes fluttered out, carpeting the ground around a dazed Fabio. Purple with embarrassment, he scrambled to his feet and began collecting the scattered banknotes, stuffing them as best he could into his pockets, at the same time trying to close the retrieved suitcase. The dozen or so passengers already on the ground looked at the scene with amazement, too polite to attempt to help the obviously flustered man, who finally seemed to have collected all the spilled currency.

Mortified at the exposure of his contraband money to the eyes of his fellow travellers, a humiliated Fabio climbed back into his seat, where he sat without raising his eyes for the next half hour, the time taken for help to arrive from the near-by town of Largs. Transportation was arranged back to Glasgow for the passengers, none of whom had sustained any physical injury during the incident. They were all shaken by the event, but none more so than Fabio, who sat silent during the hour long journey, only too well aware of the curious glances and whispered comments of his travelling companions.

As luck would have it, no cash was lost in the fall, and no questions were ever asked about the suitcaseful of money, but Fabio's confidence was completely shattered. He made no attempt to find another contact, returned all of the money to his various subscribers, made no more journeys of any kind to London and abandoned all his old haunts.

Mario in The Savoy had lost a good customer.

CHAPTER 5

Jimmy

*J*immy McKay was a lover of horses. Born in the Cowcaddens near Buchanan Street railway station just before the Great War and reared as a child in that area, as a boy he loved to watch the powerful cart horses pulling heavy loads in and out of the railway yard. His father worked as a carter in the yard and Jimmy would spend hours helping his parent groom and feed the horses. He grew to have a way with them, and it was astonishing to see the small boy manage and handle the massive animals with an adult's authority. In those days it was the expected thing for the son to follow in the father's footsteps, but Jimmy, endowed by nature with a sharp and perceptive intelligence, had started to think of other ways of making a living.

As he grew older he had become aware that his father had one bad habit; he did not squander his weekly pay packet

on drink as did most of his fellow carters, but he did like to bet on horses, and Jimmy would note with interest that although his 'auld man', as the father was affectionately referred to, seemed to pour a never-ending stream of shillings into the outstretched hand of the local street bookie, he seldom seemed to get anything back. It appeared to the young adolescent that being a bookie was a good way to make money, and mentally he quickly discarded the idea of taking up his father's trade.

As a rare treat Jimmy McKay would be taken to visit the racetrack at Ayr, where he marvelled at the sleek and graceful racehorses to be seen there, fiery and prancing, and such a contrast to the plodding percherons of the railway yard. So with his mind made up, and with his quick wit and ease with numbers, he soon gained a job as a runner for his father's street bookie.

This was in the middle thirties, at a time when cash betting was illegal, and when the street bookie had to be on the lookout not only for police raids but also for the depredations of rival gangs who might cast an envious eye on the profits to be made at a particular 'pitch', as these illegal betting sites were known. So Jimmy became hard and streetwise. He could anticipate police raids and, now grown into manhood, had the physique and courage to deal with any interlopers who dared invade his employer's territory. So indispensable had he become to his employer that after a short time as a runner he had been elevated to the status of partner in the business.

The 'pitch' was in Ferguson Lane, a narrow side street in the Cowcaddens bordering on Joe Docherty's equally lucrative hunting ground. A stone's throw from The Savoy, the shop became the natural rendezvous for Jimmy and his workers, an arrangement which suited the owner Mario very

well indeed. These bookies were good, regular customers to have, for not only did they spend well in his shop but they served also as an excellent deterrent to visits from the moochers and various kinds of hangers-on. Through the efficient use of his fists Jimmy had acquired the well-earned reputation of being a dangerous man to cross, and since The Savoy was considered part of his territory it would be a very foolish man who would dare cause any kind of trouble there.

By this time Jimmy and Mario had become good friends. They were roughly the same age, had both gone to the same Catholic school, and although completely different in background, one an immigrant Italian with parents who could speak very little English and the other the son of a Glasgow carter who probably, if the truth be told, could also speak very little English, they had much in common. Their business interests were in the same neighbourhood and they were both keen golfers, a game which they played frequently together in the mornings, a time when the day's activities for both had as yet to start.

Time passed, the thirties rolled on and war clouds began to gather over Europe. Conscription was introduced in Britain, and much to his disgust Jimmy was called up for the army. Hitler invaded Poland, Britain and France declared war on Germany and the period of the so-called Phoney War ensued. For about six months nothing much happened in the way of hostilities, then suddenly came the attack on the Maginot Line, and the British Army, with Jimmy in its midst, found itself on the beaches at Dunkirk. Then Mussolini declared war on Britain, and Mario, who until now had been free to enjoy a booming wartime trade, found himself branded an enemy alien, was promptly arrested, and transported without ceremony to a prison camp in Canada to spend the next four years there as an unwilling guest of His Majesty's Government.

More years passed, and in 1946 Mario was free once more to don his apron behind the counter of The Savoy, standing with mixed feelings as he served a populace who in wartime had considered him a mortal enemy.

One day in late 1946 the door of the restaurant opened and in walked a much decorated soldier to stand silently in front of Mario. They looked at one another for a moment, then Jimmy extended a hand to his old friend.

'Hello Mario, I heard they had let you out. Howsit going? Fancy a game of golf?' and the friendship took off as though it had never been interrupted. Wartime experiences were exchanged; Mario had not much to tell: four years of looking at barbed wire can be a bit monotonous, but Jimmy had travelled much and the medals pinned on his chest had been well earned. He had come through four years of war and many battles unscathed, but the final tale he had to tell his old friend Mario was one of the deepest woe.

He had taken quickly to a soldier's life, and after a few weeks' training he found himself in France as part of the British Expeditionary Force (B.E.F.) drawn up behind the impregnable Maginot Line. There he was made Corporal, and because of his experience in the handling of them, put in charge of a string of horses. At that time horses and mules were still being used in the army, which was only just then in the process of being fully mechanised and he enjoyed the work, evoking as it did the days spent with the cart horses of the Buchanan Street railway yard so many years ago.

But then the Maginot Line proved less than impregnable, German Panzers went through the defences like a knife through butter, Stuka dive bombers caused carnage to the men and animals of the B.E.F, and Jimmy suffered torment at the sight of his beautiful horses being slaughtered by the rain of bombs and shrapnel from the sky. He himself was

unhurt and finally found himself on the beach at Dunkirk
with the remnants of the B.E.F, waiting to be rescued by the
armada of small boats which the citizens of Britain had
mobilised to rescue their defeated army.

Reassigned, refitted and rested, Jimmy found himself
in the North African desert with the 8th Indian Division,
taking turns in chasing and himself being chased by Rommel's
Afrika Korps, until the campaign there ended with the victory
at El Alamein. Now with the rank of sergeant, he marched
with his men through the dusty hills of Sicily, to be greeted as
liberators by the inhabitants of the many towns and villages in
their path. The good citizens of Sicily greeted the Allied
invaders of their island with open arms and there Jimmy tried
to remember the few words of Italian taught him by his old
friend Mario.

'*Salute a tutti*, give Louie due, and don't mess about',
would be his greeting to the people in the various houses they
passed through in pursuit of the retreating Germans, a sally
which, although not fully understood, brought rapturous
acclaim and a popping of wine corks from the happy locals.

But the ease of the Sicilian campaign soon gave way to
much sterner stuff. The Monastery on the hill overlooking
Cassino stood impenetrable in front of the bogged down
Allied Armies. This was one of the finest natural defence
positions imaginable, and the heaviest Allied bombardment
and assaults had been unable to force the German lines. These
hills were rocky and laced with ravines, and where there had
been trees there were now only stumps blasted by shellfire,
and any buildings there had been reduced to rubble. The
Germans, who had had weeks to prepare their positions, could
man their guns in relatively secure shelter, but the attackers
had to attempt to advance across open unprotected ground in
the face of withering enemy fire. It was impossible to supply

the forward troops with ammunition and provisions. There were no paths through the rocky hillsides, and the incessant Allied bombardments had served only to make the terrain more difficult for the attacking troops.

Mules and horses would have to be used to carry food and bullets to the fighting men, and here Jimmy came into his own. The countryside behind the front line was foraged for pack animals and these were put in Jimmy's charge. In the dark of night, for movement was impossible during daylight, the horses would be loaded with supplies and led up through the debris of battle in an attempt to reach the fighting troops. Even in darkness the losses were horrendous. Enemy flares would light the night and any movement brought down heavy mortar and machine gun fire, decimating the poor animals and causing heavy casualties amongst Jimmy's men. He emerged from all this unscathed, but when the Monastery finally fell he was left shattered mentally and worn out physically by the weeks of battle he had endured on the murderous slopes of Mount Cassino. He was decorated for his bravery in the action, ordered to take care of the remaining horses and given some well earned leave for rest and recuperation.

A few miles inland from Naples stood the shattered ruins of what had been left of the town of Caserta. The Royal Palace close by had been untouched by bombing and had been chosen by the Allied Command as Headquarters for the southern Italian theatre of war, with a large part of the sprawling ornate building designated as hospital quarters. The huge country estate had been given over as a rest area for Allied troops, and there, relaxing after the stress of battle, were thousands of soldiers from a dozen nations. British Tommys and American GI's, white and black, rubbed shoulders with New Zealanders and Australians. The free French with their

savage Goums from Algeria and Morocco and their Chasseurs Alpins, Poles and Czechs and Indians all mingled together, glad to have survived the intense warfare of the last few months. They ate and drank the local wine and lazed in the sun and played interminable games of cards, betting with the wads of Occupation Lire issued by Army Command. The rate of exchange had been set at 100 lire to the pound and every man was flush with months of unspent back pay, augmented in many cases by local Italian money earned by the sale of tobacco and chocolates and other such luxuries to the locals.

Naturally resilient, a few days of good food, wine and rest had been enough to restore Jimmy. Also, while in the rest camp he had met an old friend from Glasgow, a certain Hugh Campbell, who in later years was to become an eminent maxilo-facial surgeon in the Western Infirmary in that city. Hugh had come up with a brilliant idea. These soldiers liked to gamble said Hugh, so why not give them the opportunity to bet on horse races? Jimmy's mules and horses had been put out to pasture in neighbouring fields, and he seized on his friend's suggestion. With the help of Hugh and a few other enthusiasts, a rough and ready race track was flattened out in a field, the horses and mules were graded roughly, races were organised and Jimmy proceeded to rake in thousands of lire in bets, not only from the enthusiastic soldiers, but also from scores of local civilians keen to participate in the activities.

He had not forgotten his old skills in setting odds. His winnings were considerable, and when after a few weeks of racing activity he was ordered to report to his unit he found himself in possession of a duffel bag crammed full of lire notes. What was he to do with all this money? He had already given some thought to the matter. In one of the few parts of Caserta which had not been destroyed by the fighting he had noticed a bank, and there in the manager's office he sat with

bundles of lire neatly stacked out on the astonished official's desk. The manager's protestations about the possible illegality of opening up an account for a foreign soldier were quickly dissipated by the gift of a couple of these bundles, and Jimmy left the premises with a bank book containing a balance of some 200,000 lire, which as nearly as he could calculate represented about 2,000 pounds, a significant sum indeed in those days.

The war lasted for one more year, and Jimmy took part in several other battles on the Italian peninsula, finding himself at war's end in Innsbruck, far north of his Caserta bank. In the course of these engagements he had somehow managed to lose his bank book, but he didn't worry much about that. He knew the neighbourhood in Caserta where the bank was. He had forgotten the exact name – Banco Di Something, it was, but he remembered well the unctuous little manager, Signor Scopa. So on his first peacetime leave Jimmy made his way back to Caserta to take possession of his little fortune.

He was aghast at what he found there. The heaps of ruins had been cleared, new buildings were being built everywhere, street patterns had been altered and the place bore no resemblance to the ruined town in which he had lodged his money. Through an American interpreter who was helping with the reconstruction he told his story to an unsympathetic police captain who could offer no help. He knew of no Sig. Scopa. He was probably a temporary official sent from some head bank or other in Naples, he said. The Banco Di What? How did the British sergeant expect to find a bank if he didn't know the name? Besides, the whole town was being rebuilt, and if the bank in question had been in a damaged building it very probably would have been demolished to make way for a new structure, and a dispirited

Jimmy was unceremoniously shown the door.

He spent fruitless days making a tour of banks in the district, to be met everywhere with blank stares and shrugging shoulders. Did he not have a bank book? Did he not have any document or receipt? Could he not remember the exact name of the bank? Was he sure that it was in Caserta? A defeated Jimmy returned to his unit in Innsbruck. He was demobbed a few months later and was soon back in Glasgow to regale his friends with the tale of the misplaced fortune and to pick up the reins of his interrupted career. His 'pitch' became more prosperous than ever, and the memory of his lost lire grew less painful with the passing of the years and the growth of his fortune. As a general rule street bookies were not given to ostentation; they did not care to have it thought by their punters that they were waxing rich on their losses. Jimmy however took another view and his lifestyle reflected the prosperity of his 'pitch'. He took to driving around the Cowcaddens in a white 1910 vintage Rolls Royce Landau, always with the top down if it wasn't raining. His explanation for this idiosyncrasy was simple. 'I want my punters to know that I've got plenty and that their money is safe with me. There's no danger of me ever welshing on a bet!'

In the postwar years many a holiday did Jimmy spend in Italy, visiting the scenes of bygone battles, still greeting waiters and bartenders with his '*Salute a tutti*, give Louie due and don't mess about', and telling of how he had a lot of money invested in the Caserta area, if he could only remember where.

CHAPTER 6
Peter McNulty

*P*eter McNulty was a taxi driver. He was a good car driver, but unfortunately as a taxi driver he left a lot to be desired, for you never could be sure that he would take you to the destination requested. You might ask to be taken to The Central railway station, and you would finish up at Queen Street. You might ask to be taken to the Empire Theatre and then would finish up at The King's or at the Pavilion instead. However much these trifling mistakes might irk his customers, Peter took everything in his stride with never a frown for his mistakes and nothing but a disarming smile for the stuttering and angry complaints of his hirers. In the frequent event of a complaint being lodged with his superiors, his good-natured apology was always accepted by his understanding and long-suffering employer. This was the firm of Patterson's taxis at the top of Hope Street, a large car hiring concern with about 50

cars on the road, who after a series of such errors, were reluctantly forced to demote him. Reluctantly, because Peter had been with them for a long time before the war, and as an ex-soldier with an outstanding war record, he deserved all the consideration that could be given to him now that he had returned to civvie street.

He took his removal from the taxi ranks in his stride and in the same happy-go-lucky carefree manner that he reacted to all of his other misfortunes. It was as if the capacity for a serious approach to life had been eliminated from his nature, which in fact it had been, for Peter at one time had been as serious and as diligent a person as one could have hoped to meet.

Before the war he had worked for several years for the same firm. Hardworking and serious, he was one of their best men, and had been noted down for promotion to a responsible managerial post, but then the war intervened and Peter found himself in uniform, and his skills as a driver tested in the driving of large army transport lorries. For a time he was lucky. In the North African desert vehicles all around him suffered destruction; land mines, Flak 88 shells, Stuka bombers, all took their toll of his mates, but he bore a charmed existence and not a scratch did he suffer. Not until the Italian campaign that is, where, on the Liri valley road in the shadow of the Monastery on Monte Cassino, a shell, delivered with pin-point accuracy by the German gunners from their vantage point on the hill, exploded immediately behind his lorry. The vehicle was destroyed, his co-driver killed outright and Peter suffered a serious wound to the head. His skull was badly damaged, and to protect the partially exposed brain matter inside, a steel plate was inserted just behind and above the left ear. No longer fit for military service, he returned home and to his old job with Patterson's

motors. Not that there were many taxis to be driven, as petrol shortages had severely limited the number of cars to be seen on the roads, and the ubiquitous 'Is your journey really necessary?' posters discouraged unnecessary trips by the civilians left in the cities. However, room was found for Peter in his old capacity until his lack of reliability became known, and then Peter was given a maintenance job in the garage workshop. There was no one there from the old days to notice the startling change that had come about in Peter's character. Where once he was diligent, now he was careless. His former neat and tidy appearance was no longer there. Instead he presented a markedly unkempt appearance to the outside world. His previously serious approach to life had given way to a frivolous light-hearted attitude, which attached no importance to any situation or event. All this notwithstanding he retained the same likeable quality which had gained him so many friends in the neighbourhood.

High on his list of friends were all the members of the Petri family, owners of the nearby Savoy Chip Shop. He had especially endeared himself to mamma Petri, who had always treated him as a member of the family, and who plied him with all kinds of Italian delicacies on his frequent visits to her. After his relegation to the garage workshop his earnings had dropped considerably, given the loss of the many tips given by clients whom he had not enraged by his eccentric behaviour, so he began to do odd jobs for various people. He helped with gardening, did the occasional maintenance job on motor cars, and was much sought after for wall-papering and painting, tasks at which he excelled, providing, that is, he could be depended on to finish an undertaking once started.

The Petris could always rely on him however, for there was always a plate of pasta and a glass of wine waiting for him at mamma Petri's table after a job of work, and this was

incentive enough to keep him hard at it until the job on hand was finished. On one particular occasion he had undertaken the task of painting the wooden panels of the interior of The Savoy, a job which required doing fairly frequently given the amount of splashes of food and drink they were subjected to, and in doing this he attracted the attention of Mr Groundland, an almost daily diner there. Mr Groundland was a jeweller with a shop close by in Cowcaddens Street, next to the subway entrance, whose premises also required a lick of paint. He noticed the excellent work Peter was doing, and approached him. Would he like to do a job for him when he had finished with The Savoy? Peter agreed and a few days later began work. The surroundings fascinated him. Never had he seen so many gold and silver pieces of jewellery so casually displayed, so much wealth concentrated in the one spot, and the germ of an idea began to grow in him. Mr Groundland had a good number of sovereigns laid out in these displays, and each night before closing time, the sovereigns would be collected, placed in a tray and deposited in a large safe behind the counter. Mr Groundland himself would see to the locking of the safe, and the keys would then be placed carefully in a little secret drawer set into the lip of the handsome mahogany counter which graced the centre of the shop. Over the space of a few days Peter observed these procedures gravely. His presence went unnoticed. Everyone in the neighbourhood knew Peter. He was simply part of the decor, and Mr Groundland gave not a thought to him as he went about his business shutting up the shop.

One night, when Peter's paint job was almost finished, and the sovereigns and some other pieces of jewellery all put away, Mr Groundland looked around, saw that the premises were empty, set the alarm, and went home, closing the heavy front door behind him. Some 10 minutes went by and Peter

stirred slowly from his hiding place in the staff toilets, massaging some feeling back into his cramped limbs. He chortled and whistled to himself as he crept up the steps to the main shop and did a little tap dance as he extracted the safe keys from the secret drawer. This was long before the days of sophisticated burglar alarms which could detect movement in any space, so his activities proceeded undisturbed. He inserted the key into the safe's lock, drew a deep breath, turned the key and jerked the heavy door open as quickly as he could. Ignoring the strident clanging of the alarm, he rapidly filled his pockets with handful after handful of glittering gold sovereigns. Nothing else did he touch, and with the gold coins all removed from the safe, he closed the iron door and quickly returned the keys to their rightful place in the secret drawer. He ran to the massive back door of the shop, a heavy wooden and metal affair secured with two large bolts, released them quickly, jerked the door open, and disappeared into the darkness of the back yard. The whole affair had taken no more than a couple of minutes and by the time two passing policemen had traced the ringing alarm to the jeweller's shop on their beat, Peter was well away from the scene of the crime. The policemen examined the shop. There was no sign of a break-in. The front door was secure, so round to the back they went, and discovered the door there lying ajar, undamaged.

The owner was summoned, and an anxious Mr Groundland inspected his shop. Nothing visible had been touched, no sign of a forced entry, so obviously Mr Groundland had forgotten to set the bolts on the back door before leaving the premises, allowing the door to move slightly and setting off the alarm. With a few jokes aimed at his own forgetfulness, he closed all doors properly, thanked the policemen for their prompt attention and sent them on their way, fortified with a placatory nip of his best malt whisky.

In a euphoric mood Peter walked into his favourite pub, The Glen Afton, greeted some of his cronies there, and stood them all drinks, tossing a couple of golden sovereigns on the bar in front of a startled barman in payment. Further mellowed by the alcohol consumed, he wandered round to The Savoy, enquired of his loving mamma, who promptly invited him into the back shop to partake of his favourite pasta and wine, and who gasped in amazement as he pressed half a dozen shining gold sovereigns into her hand as a parting gift. He wandered around the Cowcaddens that night, leaving behind him a trail of glittering gold wherever he happened to stop, and finally went home to sleep the contented sleep of the happy and the just.

Next morning Mr Groundland opened up as usual at 9 o'clock sharp, slipped the key from its hiding place and proceeded to open the safe. He looked with slack jaw at the empty sovereign shelf, unbelieving and uncomprehending, then immediately sprung into action. The two CID men who had answered his frantic summons questioned the shop owner closely, and within the hour the obvious suspect, Peter, sat languishing in a prison cell in Maitland Street with the 20 remaining sovereigns from the 100 he had purloined lying confiscated at the arresting desk in the police station. The CID men painstakingly retraced the prisoner's footsteps, and by the end of the day the 100 stolen sovereigns lay safely in police hands, waiting to be used as evidence in the trial of Peter McNulty. The only losers in the affair were the publicans who had exchanged good liquor for the gold coins, and the two ladies of the night who were now deprived of any compensation for the services rendered to Peter in the hours before his arrest.

His goods now safe, Mr Groundland pondered whether to press charges against Peter. The man was not a thief

in the generally accepted sense of the word, he was in all probability not responsible for his actions and no damage to property had been done. But on the other hand such behaviour could not be tolerated, so Peter was duly charged with the theft of 100 gold sovereigns.

A young and ambitious Glasgow lawyer was about to embark on a distinguished career as a criminal lawyer. As a partner in the newly formed law firm of Hughes Dowdalls, Lawrence Dowdalls had to date defended a few minor actions in the Glasgow courts, but so inconsequential had these actions been, a series of drunk and disorderlies, a wife-beating or two, some petty thefts etc., that his exceptional talents had never been fully displayed. When the accused's distraught mother presented Peter's case to his firm he jumped at the opportunity. His client was obviously guilty, he pleaded to the court. But look closely at the extenuating circumstances. The lawyer waxed eloquent in describing his client's background, with a flow of rhetoric that was soon to become famous in the courts of the land. A wounded war hero, a life blighted by injury sustained in the defence of his country, etc. etc. It was no more than the truth, and so convincingly presented as to bring tears to the eyes of many in the courtroom. Peter was found not guilty by reason of diminished responsibility and bound over to submit himself for treatment. During all these events his bubbling good nature had diminished not one whit. He sat happily throughout the proceedings: his lawyer, who had achieved instant fame in the press by his handling of the case, was thanked with a slap on the back, leaving the matter of payment up to his doting mother, and Peter returned to his carefree ways. Despite medical treatment his condition got no better. He grew to care less and less about things, his personal health included, and he took ill one winter's day and died, a belated fatality of the exploding shell on the Liri valley road 12 years before.

CHAPTER 7
Holy Oil

*I*n the years following the war, life was difficult for anyone running a fish and chip shop or restaurant. This was not because of any lack of trade, far from it, for business in general had never been so good. Industry was booming in an attempt to repair the ravages of the war years; demobbed soldiers in their thousands were returning to civvie street with pockets full of gratuity pay and money had never flowed so freely as everyone seemed bent on an orgy of spending. The lifting of the wartime blackout had revitalised the night time entertainment trade in the city centre, with pubs, dance halls and cinemas doing unprecedented business. In those days there was no superabundance of fast food cafeterias and takeaways as can be found in any city centre now, and the relatively few fish and chip shops were queued from morning until night by hungry patrons. Severe rationing of food was

still in force, food coupons were still required for delicacies such as eggs, butter and meat and the only foods freely available were fish, potatoes and bread. The time was yet to come when, in the early fifties, a critic of the new Labour post-war government was able to say (with truth) that only an organisational genius could have brought about a shortage of coal and fish on an island made of the one and completely surrounded by the other. The trouble was that although the raw materials were abundant the materials used to fry them were not. Dripping was in very short supply and severely rationed, and cooking oils were unobtainable. Every fish and chip shop had a small allocation of dripping, (the ingredient used to fry their food), and in all cases this ration, which was based loosely on pre-war consumption, went nowhere near to meeting demands. As a result many shops opened only for a few hours each day or for one or two days each week. That is, the law-abiding ones did. Others, in the great majority, sought supplies on the lucrative black market in an attempt to maximise the number of hours they could open. If you could keep your doors open you were guaranteed sales and made money.

Mario, the owner of The Savoy, had tapped in to some very rich black market dripping seams. Livestock farms on the outskirts of Glasgow did a brisk but illegal trade in the clandestine killing of cattle and pigs, thus serving two branches of the black market. The butchers would buy the meats, and fish and chip shops and restaurants would buy the rendered down meats as frying fats. Mario had a long list of such farms, and weekends would be spent touring them and filling the car boot with a variety of grades of cooking fats to be used the following week to fry fish and chips. Some farmers actually made more profit on the black market than was made in legitimate trading, with the added advantage of

there being less work to do: no records to keep, no tax returns to make, and no tax to pay. The only disadvantage was in knowing what to do with the undeclared profits. Many farmers, relatively unsophisticated in the management of capital, could think no further than putting the pound notes under the floorboards. This procedure carried unexpected dangers, and it was rumoured that one such had his entire hoard eaten up by mice! To Mario's certain knowledge one pig breeder on the outskirts of Glasgow did not trust paper money, and kept his illicit gains in the form of half crowns and two shilling pieces packed into milk urns and stored in remote barns.

Ships docking at the busy Glasgow docks were also a prolific source of black market goods. Coming as they did from more fortunate countries in the Americas which had escaped the ravages of war, goods were always in surplus, and it was not difficult to find the obliging galley cook who would sell you a half-hundredweight or so of prime Argentine beef dripping plus a 10 gallon drum of cooking oil.

All this had its element of danger, of course. If you were found in possession of black market cooking fats a hefty fine could be levied by the local food office. If, as many times was the case, the dripping and oil had originally been stolen from somewhere, then the police were involved and criminal charges could follow. Despite the obvious fact that some shops were opening far longer than their allocation allowed, possession of black market goods had to be proved, and Mario had grown adept at sticking to 'honest' black market sources, avoiding the criminal ones and outwitting the local food office. Moreover, many food offices were sometimes quite accommodating in turning a blind eye to the obvious. What harm was there in feeding a hungry public? None whatsoever, and this philosophy was shared by many a sympathetic food

office inspector in the exercise of a quid pro quo.

The Savoy was a very busy shop and Mario was ever on the lookout for new sources of cooking fats. Not only was he a hardworking lad but he was also a dutiful son who made it a point every day to visit his aged mother on his way home. Mamma Petri was a devout woman who attended Mass every day in all kinds of weather, sometimes bringing gifts of candles and flowers to the local priest, the former to be used in acts of supplication to statues of the Virgin and the Saints and the latter for the decoration of the high altar. One day, as he passed by his mother's on the way home, Mario noticed a large can of some kind of liquid on the kitchen table. On enquiring he was informed that this was a special oil sold in Catholic Truth Society shops for use in Churches where it was blessed by a priest, and then, as holy oil, would provide a floating base for candles, thus rendering them more potent as supplicatory objects. The holy oil was also used sparingly in the administration of some of the Sacraments of the Church, and Mamma Petri made it a point to keep the local church well supplied with this liquid.

Mario pondered. Was this a possible new source? What harm was there in experimenting? After all, the oil was not holy until it was blessed, so he could not see why anyone or anything on the other side of the grave could possibly object to its use for the benefit of the living. So he sent old Ivo on an errand. Old Ivo was a fixture in the back shop of The Savoy. He arrived at the crack of dawn each morning when he began to wash, peel and cut potatoes into chips, happily tending his machines, puffing on a foul pipe, listening to the wireless and running the occasional errand when asked. He would stay on all day. In the summer he went out for an occasional walk, and in the winter he was quite happy to sit in the warmth and comparative comfort of his work shop, cutting chips and

keeping his machines spotlessly clean.

A few hundred yards from The Savoy stood a Catholic Truth Society shop, and on this day Ivo was dispatched there to purchase a gallon tin of church oil. Mario would have gone himself, but since he was known there as the owner of The Savoy and not noted for his piety, his purchase of oil might have been viewed with suspicion. On Ivo's return a half pint or so of the oil was poured into one of the three cooking pans of the fish range and thoroughly mixed into the existing quantity of deep fat. A basket of chips was experimentally fried. Mario felt a surge of excitement. He had indeed struck oil. Up came the fried chips, golden brown and crisply dry, of a texture achieved only by the best fish fryers and by the best dripping. The taste matched the appearance. Deliciously tasty, dry, and without the sometimes characteristic greasy taste, these chips were undoubtedly the best Mario had ever produced. A similar amount of oil was decanted into the remaining two pans, and for the rest of the day The Savoy's customers partook of some of the best fish and chips they had ever tasted.

However, a gallon of oil does not go far, even when used in small quantities, so after three days Ivo was dispatched once more for a further purchase, and once more the resultant mix produced magnificent results. When the second gallon was exhausted Mario sent Ivo further afield. It would not do to arouse suspicion by buying from one source only, so a list of Catholic supply shops was drawn up, and Ivo was dispatched by taxi to make the necessary purchases.

Although Ivo was a man of very few words he was not devoid of intelligence, and he did remonstrate on one occasion with Mario when it became obvious to him what the church oil was being used for. Was it right to use holy oil to fry fish and chips? 'Ah but!' replied Mario, 'It's not holy till the

priest blesses it!' and with this answer Ivo was grudgingly satisfied. He was a loyal man, and the secret was safe with him.

It has repeatedly been said that The Savoy was a busy shop, and to handle this business the very best and latest fish frying range had recently been installed. This consisted of three large pans set in a stainless steel frame, the pans being fired by powerful gas jets. The fumes from the burning gas and the steam from the cooking process were carried away by a powerful fan into a metal duct which passed underneath the cement floor. The duct appeared above floor level in the back shop where Ivo worked, passed through two heavy wooden partitions and then disappeared up the back of the tenement to eject all fumes above roof level. These wooden partitions formed two of the sides of a staff lavatory. The problem with the underground duct was that it was impossible to keep clean and free from accumulations of fat and grease. It was however self-cleaning in a primitive sort of way, for every now and then, at peak periods when the heat from the gas jets became intense, the duct caught fire regularly. This served to burn out the accumulated grease, and the fire would then extinguish itself, its fuel exhausted. There was no danger of the fire spreading to the pans above. The fierce draught from the extraction fan kept the flames well away from the inflammable fats there. The roar caused by these fires, which happened regularly two or three times a week, could be quite frightening and out of all proportion to their danger, and Ivo was well used to the occurrence, and paid no heed.

One winter's day at lunch time the shop was particularly busy, and the gas jets were roaring to their full capacity. Ivo was seated comfortably on the staff lavatory seat, trousers off and hung on a hook behind the door, quite content to sit in the warmth of the little cubicle. He was reading the *Noon Record*, a betting sheet of that era, and this was

draped over the warm duct which passed through the toilet. Suddenly there was a familiar roar and the duct under the cement caught fire. For some reason or other the fire was much more intense than usual, and in a fraction of a second the duct in the toilet glowed cherry red with the heat, and the Noon Record caught fire. A few seconds later the wooden partition began to smoulder, and wisps of flame began to lick upwards from the by now red hot metal duct. From some hidden resource Ivo found the speed of youth, leapt to his feet, took no time to collect his trousers, flung open the back door and dashed into the backyard, trouserless. A heavy return spring slammed the door shut behind him.

As was always the case, the fire burnt itself out, but Mario could smell smouldering wood and rushed into the back shop, just in time to throw water on the burning wooden partition, thereby averting what could have been a dangerous fire. He went back to the front shop to attend to customers, with never a thought to Ivo. The lunch rush over, Mario went back into the workshop to inspect the damage, if any, and was attracted by a knocking at the back door. There stood Ivo, rendered more speechless than usual by his predicament, with spindly legs purple with cold .

It was all the fault of the oil, grumbled the old man through his pipe and clenched teeth. It must have been the oil that caused such a bad fire. It was a sacrilege to use it and the fire was a warning of more drastic things to come. He was finished as far as buying it was concerned. A further problem arose. His trousers were badly scorched and ruined, so he had to be given a pair by Mario. They were not easy to replace, since coupons were required for the purchase of clothing and neither Ivo nor Mario had any, but the ubiquitous black market came into play, and next day a much mollified Ivo was presented with a brand new pair of trousers by his employer.

Two days later Mario himself went into a Catholic Truth Society shop at the other side of town and asked for a gallon tin of church oil. Surprisingly, but perhaps not so surprisingly, for The Savoy was something of an institution visited by many bent on a night out in some city centre cinema, the owner recognised Mario. 'I hope you're not going to use this to fry chips,' was the remark. 'Beggar the thought,' was the quick answer, given to cover up guilt and confusion. 'I want you to send it to Father Doherty at the church of the Holy Cross.' And so ended the affair of the holy oil, with the good Father Doherty the recipient of an unexpected but nevertheless welcome gift for use in his church.

For some time afterwards The Savoy's customers were heard to complain about the fall in quality of The Savoy's fish suppers.

CHAPTER 8

The Brothers

A visitor from outer space to the Cowcaddens in the years up to its redevelopment in the early seventies might quite logically have assumed that the only liquids drunk by the inhabitants were beer, whisky and various other alcoholic concoctions for the area was awash with pubs. In just two tenement blocks in Renfrew Street there were five in all: The Camp Bar, The Atholl Arms, The Glen Afton, Dunbars, Wilsons, and The Small World. Adjacent to these in Hope Street could be found The Savoy Bar (no relation of The Savoy Chip Shop). Then further north up Hope Street, perhaps 50 yards from Dunbars, and forming part of the Theatre Royal building, came The Top Hat. Facing that, in Cowcaddens Street was Doherty's Bar, itself only a few yards away from the colourful Jock Mills Variety Bar with its gay Vitrolite frontage depicting a dancing clown. Hugh, the owner of Doherty's Bar owned

another pub further up the Garscube Road which carried the imposing name 'The Symposium', although Hugh was rather vague about why he had chosen that name. It was a safe bet to wager that the customers there could probably not pronounce the word, let alone know the meaning of it. In the rabidly sectarian Glasgow of those days the names and the decor of pubs were of the maximum importance. Green was a colour never used in drinking places with a mainly Protestant clientele, and blue was shunned in pubs frequented by those of the Roman Catholic persuasion. The classic example of what could happen if such maxims were ignored was the fate suffered by two new pubs just opened, one in Govan (a mainly Protestant district) and one in Garngad (mainly Catholic). In an attempt to modernise drinking habits and to get away from the traditional image of the get-drunk-quick, spit-in the-sawdust drinking place, the owners of the two new pubs, a chain of brewers from England who evidently did not know their Glasgow, had spent a lot of money in creating modern and comfortable bars where civilised drinking could be indulged in.

The Govan pub was named 'Three Coins in The Fountain', after the popular film of the day (filmed in Rome), and the one in Garngad bore the name 'Lochinvar'. The latter was decorated by a magnificent glass panel etched with the figure of the young Lochinvar riding a prancing stallion, which unfortunately bore a startling resemblance to the figure of King William of Orange which goes to decorate the banners of the Orange Order. Both pubs were wrecked within a few days of opening, to reopen later with less sensitive names and symbols!

The grandest, and without doubt the busiest of the Cowcaddens pubs was The McGregor, a huge barn of a place in the centre of the district. It was all a pub should be. The

windows, ornately engraved and illuminated with thistle emblems were striking and were set in a polished mahogany frontage which caught the eye from the outside. Once through the richly embossed doors a warmly decorated interior with a long broad bar and cosy booths greeted the eager drinker. Even on the traditionally quiet pub nights, Monday through Thursday, the place was well frequented, but then on Fridays (pay-day) and on Saturdays (football day) there was not a square inch of free space to be had in front of the bar, and the air was merry with the sound of ringing tills. The establishment was owned by two brothers, John and Eric McLeish. John was 10 years younger than Eric. In the sixties The McGregor had already been in the family for more than 20 years, and had been run well and harmoniously by the two brothers for that time. In the running of such a business complete honesty and trust amongst those handling the large amounts of cash which came across the counter each day is important, and the two brothers could take time off and go on holiday in the relaxing knowledge that the business had been left in secure and honest hands. The remarkable thing, however, was that the two brothers had not spoken directly to one another since the end of the war. They were avowed enemies, but the attraction of the money to be made in The McGregor was far stronger than the intensity of their emotions, and thus they continued to be partners.

Eric had married when quite young, and in the late thirties already had two children whilst John, happy to lead the life of an affluent man about town, had remained a bachelor. That is, until he met Judy, a barmaid in an upmarket pub in the West End district of Glasgow. The pub shall remain nameless. She was the perfect barmaid. Not only could she dispense drinks quickly and accurately, but her physical appearance attracted men to her bar in droves. In an era when

63

Mae West was the epitome of feminine pulchritude and the sex symbol of the day, Judy by far and away out-Maed West. She was curvaceous and luscious, she oozed sex as she moved about dispensing her drinks, and the customers would lean mesmerised against the bar, entranced by the swaying of her breasts and hips. The rule of the house was whisky and beer only to be drunk at the bar, but many a teetotaller would be happy to pay whisky prices for a glass of lemonade for the satisfaction of being able to stand and ogle her at the bar. The pub where she worked was in an area not normally frequented by John, but her fame had spread wide, and one night John decided to see for himself. He was immediately and irrevocably hooked. He stood at that bar for hours, drinking lemonade after lemonade, at whisky prices, just for the pleasure of watching Judy move around behind the bar, and hoping for the odd word or two from her as she undulated about in the course of her duties.

Judy was wise in the way of the world, and she began to pay special attention to this presentable young man who came in every other night to stand for hours drinking lemonade, his eyes riveted to her every movement. She became especially attentive once informed that her young admirer was one of the McLeishes of the famous McGregor Bar, and therefore worth a bob or two. Business being what it was she never had much time to stand and talk to customers, but she spent as much time as possible in the vicinity of young John, exchanging the odd word whilst leaning provocatively over at him. Despite his good looks, John was a shy man with the ladies, but he could see that Judy was attracted to him and so plucked up enough courage to ask the ravishing young barmaid for a date. Judy had had plenty of experience with men, she could see a good catch in the wealthy young publican, and so after a relatively short courtship she coyly

accepted his offer of marriage. And so they were married, and set up home in a bungalow in a fashionable suburb of Glasgow.

John was deliriously happy in his new situation: he had Judy all to himself to make ardent love to on his periods away from the pub, and life for him could not have been sweeter. But Judy found her new life boring after a while. She had taken a great delight in the furnishing of her new home, but soon domesticity began to pall. She had never been cut out for the role of demure housewife, and began to miss the hustle and bustle and atmosphere of her old job. This latent dissatisfaction did not have time to mature. Everyone's life was turned on end. Hitler invaded Poland, Britain declared war on Germany and within a matter of days John received his calling-up papers and found himself at Maryhill barracks being fitted out with a soldier's uniform. This created a problem at the family pub. Eric, exempt from military service because of his age (35) and because of a physical defect (he was very short-sighted), found himself alone in the running of the business.

War can be a great stimulus to trade, that is until the bombs come crashing down; everyone has a job, money flows freely and cash is spent with never a thought for tomorrow. The McGregor was busier than ever, if that were possible, and John found himself alone in the running of a two-man business. Whom could he trust at the till if he wanted some free time? The two brothers conferred and John came up with the perfect solution – Judy. She would now be alone at home, there were as yet no children, she was an experienced barmaid, and as a member of the family she could be trusted implicitly in the handling of the half crowns and ten bob notes that came pouring over the counter. So John went off to war and Judy took over at the bar of The McGregor. She was

an instant success. Customers drank an extra round or two for the privilege of standing at the bar and watching her at work, and her simmering dissatisfaction at the boredom of married life was forgotten. To a certain extent Judy missed John, but her life now was again full of interest. She basked in the lecherous admiration of her customers and did not give much thought to her absent soldier husband. She was genuinely fond of John, but her initial attraction to him had been the security his money offered. In short Judy did not reciprocate the irresistible physical magnetism her husband felt for her.

At first Eric did not have much contact with his sister-in-law. They would meet briefly at the change of shifts where the business of the day was discussed. Judy did her work well, was completely trustworthy in money matters, and Eric was perfectly happy with his new working partner. He may have been a trifle short-sighted, but there was absolutely nothing wrong with his sense of smell and sense of touch. Judy used a delicate perfume which enhanced her femininity, and her delicate fragrance aroused vague stirrings in him. The occasional touch of her hand and arm increased these until they developed into an uncontrollable passion. He threw caution to the winds, forgot that he himself was married and that the object of his desire was his brother's wife and that John was somewhere in the Middle East being shot at by Germans, and embarked on a torrid love affair with his new business partner. Judy reciprocated in kind. She was moved passionately in a manner she had never experienced with her husband, and she too thrust the thought of her marriage to the back of her mind. The war continued, occasionally John would come back home on leave quite unsuspecting, and the two illicit lovers would abstain from meeting until John was safely back at war as the target for enemy bullets.

The one fly in the ointment was Eric's wife, Lucy. For

a long time now she had realised that her husband's ardour had cooled, and the occasional trace of perfume on Eric's clothes made her certain that her husband was having an affair. Her accusations brought strong denials. Excuses were made for the faint scent on his shirts, and reasons were given for unusual absences from home. These in no way satisfied Lucy, who continued in her suspicions, but never for a moment did she suspect Judy as being the third point of the triangle. One day, after a particularly acrimonious confrontation with Eric, she decided on a course of action, and hired the services of a private detective to investigate her husband's wanderings. No more than a few days were required to bring out the fact that Eric's trail led straight to Judy's bungalow, and then all hell let loose. Lucy was a large and strongly-built woman, and instead of dissolving into a flood of tears as might have been expected of a lesser woman, she confronted the luckless Eric with the evidence and proceeded to give him a couple of black eyes and a bloody nose, promising him more of the same unless he mended his ways. Seething with anger and outraged virtue she challenged the frightened Judy with the same evidence, and only the intervention of some bystanders in the pub saved the errant wife from a beating. Mortified and ashamed, for in those days it was still a deplorable and embarrassing thing to be caught in flagrante, Judy fled the scene, never to be seen again behind the bar at McGregors. But Lucy was as yet not satisfied, still simmering with indignation and anger, and without giving a thought to any possible consequences she wrote to John to inform him that whilst he was ducking bombs in North Africa and Italy his brother and his wife were playing games of a different nature on the home front.

By this time the war was at an end, and John came home immediately on compassionate leave to attend to his

shattered domestic affairs. Afraid and ashamed to meet her husband, Judy had packed up her things and had gone to stay with her mother in a far part of Glasgow, but Eric could not avoid the righteous wrath of his brother. A mighty row ensued, and Eric was informed that he was going to be cited as co-respondent in the divorce action that was to be raised against Judy. Given the indisputable evidence of the detective, and the sympathy of the court, which lay all on the part of the deceived soldier, the action was successful, the bonds of matrimony were dissolved and Judy and John were once more free agents. Then came the question of a dissolution of partnership. The business was a valuable one. A great deal of money was required for one brother to buy out the other and, they reasoned pragmatically, where could either of them find a business with such an earning capacity if they split up? And where could a trusted partner be found to handle the cash at The McGregor for whichever of the brothers was left there?

There were lengthy consultations with the family lawyer and accountants, and finally after long and acrimonious arguments a modus vivendi was agreed upon. For a trial period the two brothers would carry on in business together but no contact other than a purely business one was to be made, and that only for a few moments each day. They agreed to ignore domestic differences for the common financial good. A much chastened Eric made peace with his wife, and John, much matured by his wartime experiences and now much more worldly wise, came to the realisation that the divorce could be classified as good riddance. Within a year he remarried, this time to a rather plain type who made him an excellent wife, and in the fullness of time presented him with three fine children. In view of the circumstances it is perhaps not remarkable to note that John's second wife, Margaret, has never met her brother-in-law.

As for Judy, she went back to her old job as a barmaid, flitted from one lover to another, and retired unmarried, a rather hard and brassy blonde. The brother's trial period in business together again lengthened into years, but they never spoke again and their strange business relationship became an established way of life. However the two brothers had one more thing in common, they both enjoyed a regular tea at Mario's Savoy. Mario, ever gregarious, became quite friendly with each one, especially Eric who was the more talkative of the two, and with whom Mario enjoyed the odd game of golf. One day in the early sixties after a game and a couple of shandies in the club house, Eric became more than usually loquacious, and Mario felt the time was ripe to ask him the question which had puzzled him for a long time. Why did the two brothers not talk to one another?

Eric swelled his chest and put on his best self-righteous churchgoing face.

'See that yin? I don't want anything to do with him. He did me a right dirty trick a long time ago. He named me as co-respondent when he divorced his wife just after the war!'

CHAPTER 9
Big Steve

*B*ig Steve Campbell was a chucker-out. Establishments which cater to the public in any manner or form and which look for some degree of control over the persons crossing their entrance sometimes employ suitably qualified persons to stand watch at their portals. The grander and more select premises, be they bank, office block, restaurant, club or hotel, use the services of a commissioner, usually a retired policeman or soldier, of suitably imposing demeanour and clad in a splendid uniform, his appearance commensurate with the importance of the establishment concerned.

Next on the social scale is the less imposingly uniformed and slightly less impressive doorman, on duty at the entrance of places such as good quality cinemas, theatres, dance halls and bars, while down at the very bottom of the scale is the bouncer or chucker-out, on guard at low class

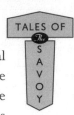

pubs, clubs and dance halls. The chucker-out wears no special uniform. Indeed, the less elaborate and expensive his attire the better, for the rate of wear and tear on clothes caused by the frequent fights and scuffles of necessity participated in by this group is very high indeed.

The Savoy Restaurant had great need of a chucker-out. During the daylight hours its clientele, which consisted mainly of shoppers and passers-by from the adjacent Sauchiehall Street area, was of impeccable behaviour, but at night the nature of the place changed. The troglodytes of the Cowcaddens began to circulate on the pavements. Drunks and prostitutes – the low-life of Cowcaddens – left the pubs at closing time and looked for the nearest chip shop to add to their alcohol-filled stomachs.

The presence of these unwanted customers was a constant source of anxiety to the owner of The Savoy, the young Mario Petri. Not only did they act as a disincentive to any prospective decent customer at that time of the evening, but their drunken and uninhibited behaviour very often spilled over into brawls and fights which would leave a trail of broken tables and chairs in their wake, not to mention the occasional bruise and contusion on the body of young Mario as he sought to protect his premises from the depredations of his unwanted customers.

These almost nightly fracas sometimes occasioned the intervention of the police, who were summoned to the scene by a series of shrill blasts on the police whistle supplied by them to Mario for use in just such a situation. There were no personal radios for communication in those days. Beats were patrolled by policemen always in twos, and no constable would ever be out of earshot of a blast on an 'Acme Thunderer', the brand name of the heavy brass whistle carried by every policeman for the purpose of alerting colleagues to the need for help.

One night a particularly nasty brawl in the centre of the seating area of the shop completely disrupted the night's business and left Mario seated sadly amidst a pile of broken crockery, disconsolately nursing a bleeding nose. He announced to the two constables who had arrived on the scene that henceforth his restaurant would close just before pub closing time. A loss of business would follow of course, but the extra few pounds of takings in the till were not worth the worry and tension of having to cope with a regular flow of drunken and belligerent customers.

Not at all, came the response from sergeant Black Alex McRae, one of the two policemen who had appeared on the scene in answer to the shrill blasts of Mario's frantically blown 'Acme Thunderer'. What was needed was a good chucker-out who would keep out the drunks and leave Mario undisturbed to attend to the needs of his decent customers. His expert advice was heeded, and as a result Big Steve Campbell appeared on the scene. He was indeed a very large man. About six feet two in height, his weight of 16 stones was made up of solid bone and heavy muscle, with not an ounce of excess fat on his frame. His face seemed hewn out of solid granite, and his craggy features were set off by a bright red, almost skinless, nose, the result of a mustard gas burn received during a German gas attack on the Western Front in the spring of 1918. In the year 1934 he was 36 years of age and worked as a coalman and carter, loading and delivering heavy bags of coal to households in the Cowcaddens district. As often as not these deliveries entailed the carrying of hundredweight sacks of coal up the stairs of tenements to each landing where he emptied the coal into coalbunkers.

His wage for this backbreaking work was all of £3 a week, so the offer of £2 plus a meal each night for standing at The Savoy door for two hours to keep out drunks and

undesirables was wealth indeed. Provided with a peaked-military-style cap by Mario, he would take up his position in front of the door of The Savoy at 9.45pm every day, and stand there menacingly and unmoveable until the 11pm closing time.

Big Steve's wage was money well spent, for tranquillity reigned in The Savoy after his arrival. Any would-be troublemaker would take one look at him and move on to safer pastures. Drunks too far gone to be impressed by his appearance and still seeking entrance to the warmth and comfort of the restaurant would be disdainfully repelled by a powerful shove, which if not at first successful, would be followed by a few well placed cuffs or punches – which invariably were.

Occasionally however, disturbances would break out inside the dining area, and these would be quickly and efficiently dealt with by Big Steve. If the offender were standing, he would approach the man smilingly, lean over as if to impart a confidence, then stamp the heavy heel of his boot with all his strength on the man's toes. The ensuing howls of anguish would then stop suddenly to be replaced by an assortment of gasping gargling noises as a sharp blow was delivered to the solar plexus, after which the culprit, now reduced from aggressiveness to an ineffective mass of jelly, would be deposited none too gently on the pavement.

If however the offender were seated and refused to go on request, Big Steve would carry out a different but equally effective procedure. Standing behind the person concerned and leaning over the man's head, two hooked fingers would be inserted into his nostrils. One hand kept the body hard pressed into the chair, the nostrils were pulled backwards until the chair tilted back on two legs and the man would sit helpless as he was dragged by the nose to the nearest exit.

Once on the pavement, the chair was kicked away, leaving the man suspended by the nostrils on two powerful fingers. He would be kept hanging thus for a few seconds, then suddenly released and helped on his way down by a sharp tap from Steve's massive fist.

The punishment meted out to offenders varied in severity according to Steve's prevailing mood. He had one interest only in life – football. He was an ardent Celtic fan and the success, or lack of it, of his beloved team determined his moods. Saturday night was the time of greatest activity at The Savoy. The pavements seethed with humanity anxious to spend the weekly pay-packet and drunks abounded. Big Steve was kept busy denying them entry. If his team had won that day then fairly good-natured methods would be employed in sending them on their way, but if Celtic had fared badly then woe betide anyone who crossed his path that night. Of special importance were the nights following a Celtic-Rangers encounter, and unfortunate indeed was the person who invoked his displeasure if Celtic had lost that day to their arch rivals. Even innocent passers-by would feel his resentment.

Every night just before pub closing time, which in those days was 10pm, Mario would go to the door and stand chatting for a few moments with Big Steve. On Saturdays the talk would invariably be of football, and one night, after a rather bad defeat of Celtic by their Ibrox adversaries, Mario stood commiserating with his doorman. A small inoffensive man approached them. He wore a cloth cap, or 'bunnet', the trademark of the working man, and sported a blue and white scarf, an article of clothing which gave the clue to his team preference.

'Where's Killermont Street Bus Station?' he asked of the two standing side by side at The Savoy door. The bus station in question was about three minutes walk away. Big Steve

looked down at the man, fixed a basilisk stare at the Rangers scarf, paused for a moment, then leaned down to address his employer:

'Tell the cunt nuthin.'

He barked from the side of his mouth and gazed disdainfully into the distance over the enquirer's head. The drunks were in for a rough time that night!

Sadly, however, Big Steve's career as Savoy chucker-out came abruptly to an end one night during a moment of tragedy. Just on closing time at Campbell's pub next door to The Savoy, a fight erupted between two rival groups of customers. Those were the days of the Glasgow gangs, the notorious San Toys, The Cumbies and The Billy Boys, whose rivalries would often result in pitched battles on the streets of their respective neighbourhoods. The activities of these gangs were mainly restricted to their own areas, but occasionally small groups would venture away from their ghettos in search of trouble in other districts, and members of two rival gangs had clashed in the pub next door.

The fight spilled onto the pavement, and soon the entire street was blocked by a mass of cursing humanity raining blows on one another with an assortment of lethal weapons: chains, broken bottles, clubs with nails set into them, open razors, anything that would inflict wounds and damage on the enemy.

The police appeared after a few minutes, and began bundling the fighting hooligans into the Black Marias which had also appeared on the scene. (Black Maria was the name given to the square, black, box-like van used by the police in those days for the transportation of prisoners.)

A common enemy identified, the hooligans stopped fighting one another and proceeded to make a common front against the policemen, and the fracas, which had been limited

to the area in front of the pub, spilled over towards The Savoy door. There stood Big Steve, until now an interested but uninvolved spectator. He was almost knocked off balance by two struggling men, one a policeman who was trying none too successfully to subdue a cursing hooligan, and as he regained his balance he glimpsed a figure running towards the two men, in his upraised hand a short wooden club, obviously aimed at the head of the struggling policeman.

Quick as a flash Big Steve clenched a fist and just as the hooligan was about to deliver a blow to the head of the unsuspecting policeman, hit the man with a powerful punch. The power of the blow, a combination of the punch and the motion of the oncoming man, was shattering. It took the man full in the neck in the region of the Adam's apple, and he collapsed to the pavement, twitching and convulsing for a few seconds. Then, he lay still with blood trickling from the side of his mouth. By this time the police had the situation under control, the unconscious man was heaved unceremoniously into a Black Maria, which then, having disgorged its quota of hooligans at the Maitland Street police station, proceeded to take the unconscious man to the nearest hospital, where he was pronounced dead, with his neck broken and his Adam's apple crushed by Big Steve's heavy fist.

No action was taken in the matter; another gang member had been killed in a gang fight, which was not an uncommon occurrence in those days, and the actual manner of the death was not made public. Big Steve's action in saving a policeman from what could have been a lethal blow had been noted by other constables and he was thanked profusely by the intended victim. But his quick action had also been noted by some gang members and he was therefore a marked man.

No longer would he be able to stand alone at the door of The Savoy: even his great strength would have been of no

avail against a quick and unexpected attack by a gang of hooligans bent on avenging their dead comrade. Such a consequence would have been inevitable, so regretfully Big Steve retired from the scene, leaving the portals of The Savoy to be defended by a sequence of other lesser mortals, whose abilities did not even begin to compare with the legend left behind by Big Steve.

CHAPTER 10
The Polis

*M*aitland Street police station, headquarters of the Northern Division of the Glasgow Police, was situated a few hundred yards north of The Savoy, at the top end of Hope Street.

There was not a policeman there who had not at one time or another made use of the establishment's back shop for the occasional fish supper and quiet smoke during their tour of duty. The Savoy was ideally situated for that purpose, for at the pavement's edge of the Hope Street entrance stood a police box, a structure not seen in these days of mobile phones. (The police box gave the constable on the beat telephone access to their headquarters.) Sixty years ago the only means of communication between policemen in a given area was by means of an Acme Thunderer a whistle used by them to summon help in a crisis situation. Contact with their base was made only through phones installed in the police boxes,

which were strategically situated every few hundred yards or so. These boxes were made of concrete and similar in shape to the phone boxes of today. In size, however, they were much larger and could accommodate three or four people. They were also used to lock up unwilling prisoners awaiting the arrival of a Black Maria to take them to the cells in Maitland Street. The heavy wooden doors of the police boxes were distinguished by well-worn and clearly defined indentations at head height, occasioned by the use of prisoners' heads as battering rams to open them, a practise well calculated to impress upon the victim the clear message as to who was in charge of the situation. Similar indentations were to be seen on the swing doors of the Maitland Street station, also caused by the frequent use of prisoners' heads to push them open. No nonsense in those days about civil rights and careful treatment of offenders. If you fell foul of the law and resisted arrest then you took the consequences – a crack on the head with a baton, or even more painful, a crack with the same weapon on the ankles, followed by a cuffing around the ears – with a promise of much more to come. Such treatment was usually enough to convince even the most recalcitrant of prisoners that it was much wiser not to question the majesty of the Law. This majesty was made manifest by the appearance of many of the policemen of those days, for the physical requirements for acceptance to the force were much more stringent than they are now. The minimum height of applicants was set at 5 feet 10 inches. The great majority of the beat men far exceeded this height, and their tall brawny appearance was enhanced by the wearing of the regulation helmet of the day, which added another 10 inches or so to their already formidable image.

The slums which at that time formed an arc around the commercial heart of the city, both north and south of the Clyde, were breeding grounds for the infamous gangs which

had helped to make the city notorious for its lawlessness. Each district bred its own brand of group hooliganism: the Gorbals had its Cumbies gang; Bridgeton had The Billy Boys, Shettleson had The Baltic Fleet and Govan its Kelly Boys. These gangs were split along religious lines and reflected the sectarian bigotry of that era. The Norman Conks, a south-side gang, represented the Catholic hooligan element of the city. The Govan Billy Boys (named after King William of Orange) were their mortal enemy, and each did their best to disrupt the other's frequent processions and marches through the streets.

July was the traditional marching month for the Orange Order, and The Billy Boys drum and flute band, playing rousing Orange airs and preceded by a prancing Drum Major, would lead these processions down predominantly Catholic streets where The Norman Conks held sway. Invariably outnumbered (the ratio of Protestant to Catholic was about two to one in Glasgow), The Conks would man the windows and roofs of their fortress-like tenements and bombard the marchers below with a variety of missiles.

Bags of ordure, bricks and bottles, some empty, some filled with urine, would rain into the procession below, scattering the marchers and giving rise later to pitched battles in the streets.

These were very hard times for the police in Glasgow, and very worrying times for the good citizens of that city, who no longer felt it safe to walk the streets. So the Sheffield crime buster, Percy Sillitoe, was appointed Chief Constable and he proceeded ruthlessly and efficiently to break the power of these gangs. His methods were, to say the least, robust. He picked the roughest and toughest men in the force, formed them into so-called Heavy Squads, and gave them a completely free hand with whatever means they cared to use against street hooliganism. About 50 or so of these Heavies would be quickly

transported in plain vans to the scene of a street fight, where they were unmerciful in their use of fist and baton against the hooligans. Always they sought out the leaders for special treatment and very often inflicted injuries serious enough to put them out of action for a very long time. As has already been said, there was no such thing as a Council for Civil Liberties then, and the punishment meted out by the police more than suited the crime. Percy Sillitoe completely broke the power of the gangs with his tough methods, remained as Chief Constable from 1931 to 1943, and was knighted for his services to the community. Although the organised gangs no longer existed, his methods were continued in the treatment of the casual hooligan and criminal. From that time on, woe betide any hooligans or neds, as they were called, who caused any trouble in the streets or in any public place. Summary justice would be handed out by 'the polis' in the form of a series of heavy blows with fists, boots and batons, with any resulting marks or scars on the prisoners being attributed to the resistance of arrest on the part of the wrongdoer.

One of the finest and most feared exponents of this technique was Big Robert McKenzie, or Big Hitler, as he was called by the denizens of the notorious Garngad Road. This area was notorious for its neds, and the hard men of the area were kept well subdued by the even harder Big Hitler. He shared with Alex McNair of the Northern division the distinction of being the biggest and toughest polis in the city, and to see Big Hitler in action was an awe-inspiring sight. He could take on and subdue any four normal men by dint of hammer blows from boot, baton and fist, and was the scourge of the neds and hooligans, who dispersed hurriedly from their stations at the various street corners at the first sign of the approach of their nemesis.

One day a group of these hooligans decided that

enough was enough, and that their enemy had to be taken care of. His routine was well established. A march along the Garngad Road was always followed by a visit to the back shop of his favourite cafe for some form of refreshment, and then his route would be retraced, with occasional forays into side streets in search of suitable candidates for arrest or for disciplinary measures. Assembled in the top storey house were five neds who had been frequent targets for his displeasure. They had prised the kitchen grate from the wall and had lifted it precariously on to the window sill, ready to be dropped on the unsuspecting constable. The heavy mass of iron was released just as Big Hitler passed below the tenement window. The five delinquents had obviously never studied the theories of Newton and Galileo, for the grate was pushed out of the window just as their target was directly underneath the 50 foot drop, the result being that the lethal mass of iron hit the pavement with a terrific thump about six feet behind their target. Startled by the bang, Big Hitler looked up, saw some heads looking out of the top storey window, drew his baton and charged like an angry bull into the close and up the stairs, bent on revenge. The five neds, stricken with panic at the failure of their attempt, rushed in disarray down the steps, to be laid stiff by five mighty blows from Big Hitler's baton, and were later bundled, bloody and dazed, into a Black Maria.

The big policeman had one weakness, however. He was a staunch Rangers supporter, not that there is anything wrong with that, but his support for the Ibrox team was accompanied by an intense hatred for the Celtic green and anything associated with it. It so happened that the Garngad area was staunchly Celtic in its religious affiliation, and this no doubt was a factor in the mutual enmity which prevailed there. This dislike for the green manifested itself more than on any other time at Rangers-Celtic football matches, and it could

not have been coincidence that all his arrests at disturbances during these games consisted of green-scarfed supporters.

One Saturday whilst on duty at the Celtic end of the park during one of these hotly contested games, the score stood at 1-0 for the hated greens, and Big Hitler was beside himself with disappointment and chagrin. Suddenly at the last minute of the game a Rangers player scored, making it 1-1, and an overjoyed policeman, overcome with relief and joy, took off his helmet and began waving it around his head as exuberantly as any other Rangers supporter. The day had been wet and drizzly and the helmet was slippery: it flew out of his hand to fly in an arc into the middle of the silent Celtic supporters, never to be seen again. From then on, his normally tolerant superiors saw to it that during the encounters he would be put on traffic duty and far away from the scene of football action. He did have a grudging sense of humour however. Whilst visiting the Northern division he would occasionally accompany a colleague into the back shop of The Savoy for a nourishing plate of chips. On one occasion, since his religious predilections were well known, a daring member of staff served up a portion of chips laid out on the plate in the shape of the sign of the cross. The flicker of what could have been a smile was seen to pass over Big Hitler's face.

The Cowcaddens, served by the Maitland Street station, was one of the best policed areas in the city. Each beat was carefully patrolled by constables, always in twos, who made sure that the peace was kept in the area under their supervision, and no constables were better equipped physically to deal with any outbreak of trouble than were two habitually paired together, Alec McNair and John McSween. Big John and Big Alec were massive men by any standard. Both well over six feet in height, approaching seven feet with helmet and each weighing about 16 stones in weight, they

were an awesome sight as they strode ponderously and majestically side by side along the pavements of their beat, left thumb tucked into their belt and right arm swinging with authority in time to their measured step. They had served for two years in Sillitoe's Heavy Squad, and when transferred to normal police duties had continued to apply the techniques learned from him in their treatment of wrongdoers.

There was seldom any trouble on their beat. Once word got around that Big John and Big Alec were on duty, any would-be troublemaker would try to become as unostentatious as possible so as to avoid the summary justice meted out by these two stalwart examples of the Glasgow polis. They were both firm believers in teaching by example, and each night at the beginning of their shift a demonstration of what offenders could expect was made. At pub closing time when the police night shift began it was never difficult to find someone in breach of the law. The pubs of the Cowcaddens spilled out their nightly quota of drunks, and pavement brawls were common occurrences. These disturbances were sought out eagerly by the two companions. Suitable candidates for arrest would then be chosen, heads would be rammed against police box doors, Black Marias summoned, and dazed prisoners decanted unceremoniously into police cells. Notice had been served that Big John and Big Alec were on the job.

The example to other potential wrongdoers having been set, the two policemen would retire from the scene for a couple of hours for a quiet smoke and snooze in the back shop of The Savoy, an arrangement actively encouraged by the owner, for it gave him the certainty of quick police intervention in the event of any trouble breaking out. This was a very remote possibility, for the habits of the Big Two were known to the local hooligans, who steered well clear of the place. Then at midnight, closing time for The Savoy, they

would take a turn around their beat, check that all premises were secure, make two or three more arrests of drunks or loiterers to impress the station superintendent of their devotion to duty, then return to the pavements to amble contentedly from shebeen to shebeen, looking for the odd drink or two and always finding one or two final arrests to top off the night's work.

Crime in those days was uncomplicated. There was no car theft (there were very few private cars on the road then), vandalism was unknown and armed robbery unheard of, although safe-breaking (it was the practise in the days before electronic burglar alarms for each shop to be equipped with a safe to keep the day's drawings), was a popular occupation amongst professional criminals. Murders in the general population were extremely rare, and when one did happen it would be headline news for days on end. So frequent are murders now that unless one is a spectacular multiple affair with sexual overtones they barely merit a few paragraphs in a centre page of the newspapers. The frequent breach of the peace in pub, street bookies' pitch or fish and chip shop and cafe, the occasional house-breaking incident, and the not infrequent wife-beating complaint just about made up the complete spectrum of crime in Glasgow in those distant days. Big Alec and Big John were always ready to champion the weaker sex (unless of course they happened to be streetwalkers, in which case they were run in) and were always prompt to attend to a wife-beating call. The offender was very rarely charged in court. It could be taken as read that after the tanking administered on the spot to the aggressor in such cases the offence would not soon be repeated .

The two remained inseparable companions on the beat for almost eight years until nemesis caught up with Big Alec one winter morning. His shift had just finished at seven

am and he was on his way home after a very successful night's work that had seen no less than eight prisoners deposited in the cells. He had within him the warm glow of several whiskies partaken of in a particularly welcoming shebeen, and had not a care in the world as he looked forward to a few hours in his warm and comfortable bed. His home was only a few hundred yards from the Station, but as he passed in front of a row of four shops he came to a sudden halt.

Through the window of a newsagent's shop he could see the light of two electric torches moving towards the front door of the premises which had been left slightly ajar. Quick as a flash he drew his baton, pressed himself against the wall of the shop beside the door, and as the two burglars came through he laid them low with two powerful blows from his baton. Unknown to the policeman, the two had an accomplice stationed on the roof of the shop as lookout, and as Big Alec stepped back to admire his handiwork in the shape of the two unconscious thieves, the third man jumped down on the constable's head, kicking out with all his strength as he came to the end of the 10 foot drop. Thrown to the ground by the impact, Big Alec was half-stunned by the blow, but retained a hold on his baton. He lashed out at his assailant's legs, and succeeded with the single blow in breaking his attacker's knees. He then tried to rise from the ground, but felt a strange numbness in his legs and could only lie there with the three bodies, one screaming in pain, and the other two still unconscious. He could still manage to blow his whistle however; the blast from the Acme Thunderer carried far and was heard at the nearby police station. Help was soon at hand. The three burglars were shovelled up and put in a cell, with scant regard for their injuries, and Big Alec was taken to the Royal Infirmary. There he lay for nearly six weeks recovering from a dislocated vertebra.

He recovered, but some permanent damage had been done, and he was left with a pronounced limp. He could no longer walk a beat but was commended by the Chief Constable for his bravery and returned to duty to finish his career as turnkey in the Maitland Street station. His hands and arms had remained as powerful as ever, a fact which could be attested to by the many toughs and hooligans who felt their weight when propelled through the iron doors of the cells.

His partner, Big John McSween, was devastated by the loss of his long-time partner. He was given a series of new partners, but none of them could match up to Big Alex. He soldiered on for one more year, then retired from the force. The pavements of his beat had become his roads to Damascus, for he spent the rest of his working life surprisingly as a paid officer in the Salvation Army.

CHAPTER 11

Willie Dickie

*D*irectly opposite The Savoy Cafe was The Savoy Cinema, which had been converted into a picture house in the twenties from a theatre of the same name. From this theatre the newly opened fish and chip shop at the opposite corner had taken its title, and as the little shop expanded in size over the years to a seating capacity of well over a hundred, its fame spread to the dozens of places of entertainment in the immediate vicinity. Within a 200 yard arc towards Sauchiehall Street were three of Glasgow's most famous theatres, The Royal, The Empire and The Pavilion, together with half a dozen or so cinemas, The La Scala, The Gaumont, The Regent, The Savoy, The Paramount, The Green's Playhouse, and The Cosmo, to name but a few. All of these have now gone, with the exception of the Cosmo, which is now the GFT, and the Paramount, which is now an Odeon cinema.

From the frequenters of these dream palaces came

many of The Savoy's customers, and many too were the artistes from the three theatres who made The Savoy a regular eating-place. Jack Anthony and Dave Willis, two of Glasgow's most popular comedians in the immediate post-war years, ate there regularly. G.H. Elliot, the 'chocolate-coloured coon' of Lily of Laguna fame (just imagine what the race relations people would have to say nowadays about such a title!) regularly had his breakfast of two poached eggs on toast and a pot of tea there when on his frequent appearances at The Glasgow Empire, and many of the supporting casts from the various shows would take home a carry-out supper to their digs in Garnethill, in those days a bed and breakfast area much favoured by show folk.

A very popular yearly summer revue at The Theatre Royal in the fifties, and which appeared there regularly for more than a decade went by the name of *The Half Past Eight Show*. One of the principals was a baritone, William Dickie, a fine singer who had studied in Italy under Beniamino Gigli and who had been declared by the famous tenor to be the best non-Italian singer of Italian opera he had ever heard. *The Half Past Eight Show* ran each summer for about two months in Glasgow, and from the first arrival of the revue there William Dickie became a daily visitor to The Savoy .

He enjoyed conversing in Italian, which he spoke fluently, and from the very beginning he and Mario became firm friends. They shared a common love of opera, and more important still they were both golf fanatics, a game which they played together two or three times a week, in the mornings, before the start of their respective labours. Indeed, so keen were they both about the game that occasionally their labours took second place. In 1953 the great golfing legend Ben Hogan came to compete in the Open at Carnoustie, so at the crack of dawn one Thursday morning Willie Dickie and Mario took off

in a car to watch their hero in action over those historic links. Motor cars were much more liable to breakdowns then than they are now, and a series of minor mechanical failures lengthened the return journey so as to make the two very late back. In Mario's this did not matter much; he had a well-trained staff who could cope alone for a spell; but Willie Dickie's unexpected absence at the opening curtain brought down on his head the wrath of the stage manager, who had been forced to make some very inartistic changes to the continuity of his revue. However, Willie Dickie looked forward to his yearly Glasgow summer show for two reasons; his golf with Mario and his conversations with Roman Sauschek.

Roman Sauschek was a daily visitor to The Savoy. An ex-officer in the now disbanded Polish Army, he had been one of the flood of Polish refugees forced to make Scotland his home at the end of the war. Ironic indeed was the fact that the Nazi invasion of Poland had been the spark which had ignited that war, a war which had ended with Russian forces occupying that very country which the Allies had been sworn to liberate from the Nazis.

Because of the Russian occupation the thousands of Poles who had fought to free their country could not return there at war's end, so the British Government allowed these ex-soldiers to settle as welcome immigrants in the UK.

Glasgow and the west of Scotland played host to thousands of them. These expatriates were readily identifiable by their garb and by their behaviour. They all seemed to dress in long light coloured raincoats, carry flat briefcases under one arm and they always seemed to be in a perpetual hurry. These idiosyncrasies were seized upon by stage comedians of the day, and in every variety show the appearance of a raincoated brief-case-carrying individual, who spoke fractured English, was always good for a laugh.

Roman Sauschek sported a raincoat, always carried the obligatory briefcase, but contrary to the stereotype described above, was never in a hurry. He spent hour after hour in The Savoy, drinking interminable cups of coffee and smoking innumerable cigarettes fixed ostentatiously in a long ivory holder. Each cup of coffee was laced liberally with vodka from a large flask which he carried in a hip pocket; a veritable horn of plenty, for it always seemed able to produce as much spirits as required in the course of the day. He was a graduate in Science and Engineering from Warsaw University, spoke several languages, and could speak with authority on many subjects, particularly art and music.

He was too an inventor of sorts, and afforded his long hours in The Savoy thanks to the income generated by a gadget he had patented and which was developed by Howdens, a local Cowcaddens engineering firm. Sauschek's invention consisted of a hydraulically-controlled expanding cylinder which could be accurately calibrated to serve as a time controlled opening and closing mechanism. Howdens employed him to supervise production of his invention, and since this needed only about an hour's work each day he was free to do as he pleased for the rest of the time. The Savoy was close to Howdens, and since it counted many interesting characters from all walks of life among its clients Sauschek made his headquarters there, holding court for hours on end, discussing the events of the day and life in general with whomever of interest happened to be on hand. Mario did not mind this, indeed he welcomed it. Roman's opinions on all matters were invariably well-informed and interesting, the characters attracted to his table were colourful and verbose, and what was very important too, they consumed gallons of coffee in the course of their animated discussion, all of which helped swell profits.

Sauschek was very knowledgeable in matters of art

and music, and it was on this last subject that he and Willie Dickie used to hold endless conversations. The Pole had an amazing ear for music: once for a bet he had listened to the BBC Home Service for two hours, which at that time broadcast classical music only, and had correctly identified the composer of every piece played, much to the amazement of all present. In the field of art, Roman would boast of the second prize he had once received for a modernist painting he had submitted to an exhibition of modern art in Warsaw in the middle thirties. Then a student at Warsaw University, he had presented an interesting composition for evaluation. With the help of a shovel and pail he collected a sizeable quantity of fresh horse dung from the city streets. This he flung haphazardly on to a canvas suitably treated with glue to hold the manure, and when the mess had set, had sprayed the pattern with a variety of coloured paints. The composition was imposingly framed and hung, without a title, in the exhibition gallery. The painting was studied carefully by the panel of judges and considered to be worthy of second prize. On presentation of his award he was asked to name the painting. The next day a small plaque appeared on the wall next to his brainchild.

'*Scheiss Am Wand*' (Shite on the Wall) read the caption! The reaction of the adjudicators is not on record! Roman's ear for music comprised as well an ability to pinpoint accurately the identity of singers from gramophone records. Mario was the proud possessor of an imposing collection on wax of various operatic artistes, sometimes having as many as half a dozen tenors and baritones singing the same aria, and this would give rise to animated arguments between Roman and Willie as to the relative merits of singers such as Gigli, Tito Schipa, Lauri-Volpi, Jorling, Del Monaco, etc., in the rendering of the same piece.

Roman, however had never heard Willie Dickie sing in

the flesh. He had listened to several of his recordings, but Roman had never taken the few steps across to The Theatre Royal to hear his friend perform on the stage, despite Willie's continued invitations to do so.

'Panje', he would say to Willie (he called everyone Panje, Polish for mate or chum), 'Panje', waving his ivory cigarette holder elegantly at arm's length, 'I am not wasting my time listening to garbage music', referring to the popular songs performed by Willie in the revue.

'When you are deciding to sing somet'ing wit' musical wort', then I will come to listen.'

So one day Willie appeared in The Savoy to acquaint Roman with the good news. That week he would include the prologue from I *Pagliacci* in his performance. Now, the aria in question is a tenor aria, but because of its range is frequently rendered by baritones in the course of recitals. It is also popular enough to be enjoyed by a musically unsophisticated audience, yet, reasoned Willie, serious enough to entice Roman into the theatre to hear him sing. Roman listened gravely to this information and pondered for a while, sipping his vodka coffee and fingering the ivory cigarette holder.

'OK Panje; I will come to hear you. But I am not sitting for hours to hear garbage. Tell me vot time you are singing and I vill come to stage door and you vill arrange for me to come in and I vill listen .'

So it was agreed. Willie notified the stage door attendant that a friend of his would be presenting himself that night, and would he please escort him to the wings for his performance. Roman waited at his table in The Savoy for the designated time to come around, chatting to his friends, brandishing his cigarette holder and drinking cup upon cup of coffee, each one liberally laced with generous helpings of vodka poured from his seemingly bottomless flask. He made a

great show of consulting his wristwatch, and finally heaving himself upright, drained his cup, put away the ubiquitous holder and walked somewhat unsteadily to the door with the gait characteristic of those who have had a fraction too much to drink. 'Dosvidania, Mario, I now go to hear Villie.' and made off in the direction of the theatre.

This was The Savoy's busy time and Mario was not able to consult Roman, who by now had returned to resume his customary position at his table. When at last he could find the time to ask him how the performance had gone, a pensive Roman raised an admonishing hand. 'Ve vill vait for Villie to come.'

Some more time passed, and finally the door opened to admit a somewhat breathless Willie, traces of greasepaint still on his face.

'Well Roman, what did you think?'

Roman looked at him solemnly, drank from his cup, produced a cigarette, fitted it to the ivory holder, lit up and slowly, inhaled. 'Panje my friend, I am telling you, I have listened to opera in Warsaw, I have listened to opera in Paris, I have listened to opera in Rome, I have listened to opera in London, but never, never, never have I heard anything so atrocious. Panje, my friend, I am telling you the truth, I am making better noises with my backside than you are making tonight with your mouth on the stage!'

And he took him note by note through his performance, pointing out mistakes and inadequacies in the rendering of the aria. A chastened but nevertheless still goodnatured Willie listened and then had to agree.

'Right enough, Roman, I wasn't at my best tonight,' and took no umbrage at Roman's forthright criticism. Indeed, fortified by several nips from Roman's flask, he joined in the general merriment and they finally parted still the best of friends.

Entertainment trends change and after a few more years The Royal became an STV studio, and The Half Past Eight Show was a thing of the past, as were William Dickie's visits to Glasgow.

With the passing of the years Roman Sauschek took more and more to the flask, did no more creative work and finally died young of a massive heart attack.

Willie Dickie successfully continued with his career as a singer until well into his sixties, then set up a school of music in London, which acquired a great reputation and was much sought after by aspiring young operatic singers. He has a line of criticism which always raises a laugh among his students: 'Really, really, there are times when I make better noises flatulently!'

CHAPTER 12

Toni

*T*oni was a frequent visitor to The Savoy and Mario always enjoyed and always managed to find time for a chat with him. They conversed in Italian. Although they were both bilingual, and English came just as easily to them, for some reason Italian was their choice. Perhaps it was because of the fact that they had been, each in a different way, prisoners of the British, and the use of their native language reflected their wartime experiences. Perhaps too it might have been the strange manner of their original meeting, because for many months Mario had no idea that Toni spoke both languages.

Mario had been born in Italy, brought to Britain as a baby, and had become effectively bilingual, as only Italian had been spoken at home. His family had set down permanent roots in Glasgow, and here Mario had grown up, in a sort of limbo-land of loyalties, with a sense of belonging neither to the Italian culture of his family nor to the Scottish one of his environment.

On the day of Mussolini's declaration of war, Mario, as an Italian national, had been immediately arrested, and after a series of events which have been recounted elsewhere, found himself in an internment camp in Canada, of all places, where he remained until his return home in late 1943. It was a condition of his release that he should undertake 'work of national importance', which in his case consisted of agricultural work on a nearby farm. From time to time, at harvests and at other labour intensive periods, lorry loads of Italian POWs were taken to the farm from a nearby POW camp situated on the Gareloch, and on these occasions the farmer found Mario's fluency in Italian invaluable, for his orders could now be conveyed accurately to the prisoners without the need for a dumb mime. Mario sympathised with these POWs. It was not so long ago that he too had been behind barbed wire, and he could understand their feelings and desires only too well. During these periodic visits he got on particularly well with Toni, a quietly spoken soldier who claimed to come from Cassino and who had been taken prisoner at the battle of El Alamein. Toni seemed to be better read, better educated and far better spoken than the run-of-the-mill private from the southern regions of Italy, and Mario found conversation with him interesting and stimulating.

To make travel to and from his work easier, and with the sponsorship of his employer, Mario was granted permission by the police to own a bicycle. He revelled in his new found mobility. One Sunday he decided to cycle out to the Italian prison camp by the shores of the Gareloch to pay a visit to his new friend Toni, who had not been sent out to the farm for several weeks. By this time Italy was out of the war, the Italian POWs were now no longer enemies and the strict

TALES OF
The
S
A
V
O
Y

wartime discipline of the camp had been relaxed to allow them visitors and a degree of fraternisation with the locals. As the two sat, smoking and chatting, a pretty girl approached, also on a bicycle. She stopped in front of the two and greeted Toni with a wave and a smile:

'Hello Toni, I've brought you some home baking.'

Toni broke off his flow of Italian to Mario and replied in faultless English, with a trace of a Welsh accent:

'Thanks Betty, that's nice of you, I want you to meet my friend Mario.'

Mario's jaw sagged to the ground and he looked open-mouthed at his friend, speechless. Overcoming his astonishment he said to him in Italian, 'Jesus, Toni, why didn't you say you could speak English?'

'There was no need. We got on perfectly well in Italian, and when the war was still on I wasn't keen for anyone to know that I could speak both languages.'

With introductions over, Betty's presence was explained. She was a Land Army girl who had met Toni when the latter had been put to work alone on a nearby farm, and the Italian prisoner and the girl from Edinburgh had struck up a friendship. The three chatted together for a moment, but the atmosphere was slightly strained. Mario found it difficult to make himself speak English to Toni, who seemed to speak the language as though born with it, so he made his excuses and cycled home, more than slightly miffed that his friend had seen fit to deceive him. Several weeks went by, and with his annoyance now vanished, and curious to know the story of Toni's fluency in English, Mario cycled out to the Gareloch. Toni was no longer there. The camp was being wound up, and his friend was in one of the groups who had been repatriated to Italy.

Years went by. Mario returned to manage his own shop, The Savoy, which had been kept going by his parents

during the war years. He married and began to raise a family and he forgot all about Toni. That is, until one afternoon when the door opened and into the shop walked a familiar but nearly forgotten figure, arm-in-arm with a pretty woman and carrying a child in his arms.

'Good God! Toni!'.

'Hello Mario! Do you remember Betty? This is our little daughter Sylvia. We're married, and I'm now living and working in Edinburgh. I remembered the name of your cafe, and we thought we'd come through to Glasgow to see how you had finished up after the war.'

They chatted on about generalities, and Mario's curiosity about Toni's background was slowly rekindled. Why could the ex-Gareloch prisoner speak English so perfectly and with a Welsh accent? Where had he really come from? He did not presume to start questions with Toni's wife present, but Toni could sense the stifled curiosity and took his leave with a promise to return soon during one of the many business trips he was now scheduled to have to make to Glasgow.

Some weeks later he reappeared alone and the two settled down over a coffee. Without waiting for his companion's questions to start, Toni started immediately.

'I know you must be wondering about me, Mario, and as to why I didn't let on I knew English.'

He passed over a business card. The surname was not the one Mario had known him by five years or so ago as a prisoner on the farm.

'That's my real name, Mario. I'll tell you a story now. I know you won't repeat it, and even if you did I would deny it.'

He sipped his coffee, marshalled his thoughts and began his tale.

'I was born in Udine, but when I was about a year old my parents emigrated to Llandudno in Wales. I grew up and

went to school there. I was the only one in the family, no brothers or sisters, and at home we spoke only Italian, so I grew up bilingual and it made no difference to me which of the two languages I spoke. Funny thing, I don't think I ever in my life spoke a word of English to my parents, although they were both not too bad in it. It was just the natural thing to do. Life wasn't too easy for them: they just couldn't mix with their neighbours. Nobody ever bothered them. The people were quite friendly, but they were different to my folks in their ways. They were Protestant and in those days I think they looked on us like something strange. I had lots of Welsh pals and I was quite happy at school even though my parents were that bit different. Around about 1934 my mother was desperate to go back to her little village near Udine. It didn't matter to her that life was a whole lot poorer there – she just wanted back, so my dad packed in his job as a terrazzo worker and we went back to live in Udine. I was 14 at the time and I slotted in quite well in Italy. The language was no problem and I did quite well at school. I got a degree in languages and started teaching English at a local school until I was conscripted into the army just before Mussolini declared war on Britain.

'Because of my university degree I was given the rank of Lieutenant and posted to a counter-intelligence unit in Rome, where I had to translate documents from Italian to English and vice versa. It was a cushy posting. I might as well have been working in an office, and the flashy uniform I wore made a big hit with the birds along the Via Veneto at night. That didn't last long though. The war had begun to go badly for Italy. We got well pasted in North Africa (the Germans sent the Afrika Korps there), and the top brass decided that rather than fiddling with bits of paper, my talents could be put to better use with our army in the desert. So I was posted to the

Folgore division stationed at Tobruk, and there I began to interrogate British soldiers captured in the various desert skirmishes. Our High Command were badly in need of information about British troop movements and dispositions. The RAF had complete command of the air, and any observation planes we sent over were 100 per cent certain to get shot down. The Italian divisions and the Afrika Korps were really fighting blind, with very little knowledge of what was happening behind the patrol encounters that occurred in the desert every day. Those British, Australian and New Zealanders I interrogated were good soldiers, and well coached by their officers. Not a scrap of information did they give out, even when we used the most sophisticated verbal interrogation techniques we knew. Funny thing about the war in North Africa. Prisoners were never beaten up to get information out of them. Not on either side. I heard of some of the things that happened in Yugoslavia and Greece and were happening in Russia to prisoners to get them to talk, stories that would make your hair curl. We were given orders to treat prisoners hard but properly. It cuts both ways, I suppose. They had a lot more of ours than we had of theirs, and anyone who started any rough stuff would just be calling much of the same on their own lads.

'Anyhow, one day I was called to military headquarters at Tobruk. A Colonel Piovani and some other officers were there. My fluency in English had been noted, said the Colonel. Was it true that my speech was indistinguishable from that of a native-born Briton? I had to answer in the affirmative. I was going to be asked to volunteer for a very dangerous task, he continued. We were absolutely in the dark about British troop dispositions, he said, and we desperately needed some intelligence, some eye-witness observations, done on the ground. Would I be willing to put on a British uniform, to be

dropped off somewhere behind enemy lines, to make any observations I could, then be picked up after a few days with whatever information I had been able to gather? The idea was not as crazy as it sounded. Battles in the desert were sometimes chaotic and very fluid. Most encounters took place between highly mobile armoured groups, and it was no uncommon thing for individual soldiers to be separated from their companions and wander round the desert in search of their unit. If I were given the proper uniform and authentic papers, could I pull off a deception? Could I pretend to be a British soldier, a junior officer, say, in search of his unit?

'Could I wander around and pick up all the information I could, then rejoin the Italian lines? I had to realise the danger. If my deception were uncovered I would be shot out of hand as a spy. I thought long and hard about it. It was a challenge really. My English, with its touch of Welsh accent, could pass anywhere. My appearance, given my northern Italian parents, was more Nordic than Latin, and I had absolutely no doubt that I could pass muster on these two counts. But would I have the nerve to keep up such a deception in what were bound to be nerve-wracking circumstances? Piovani sat through the moments of my silence. I'll understand if you refuse, he said. This is not normal soldiering, but any information you might be able to get would be of great importance and could help to save many of our soldiers' lives. When you're young and haven't any ties you can do some daft things, and when I think about it now I get the shakes, but about two weeks later I was sitting in a small caterpillar-wheeled troop carrier, kitted out in the uniform of a British Lieutenant.

'Round my neck was an identity disc bearing the name 'Thomas Martin', and in my tunic pocket were documents identifying me as belonging to the 13th Corps of

the 8th. Army. I knew a lot about Lieutenant Martin. He had been captured whilst on patrol some weeks before, had been thoroughly interrogated by me, and was now sitting out his time in a POW camp in Sicily, slightly mystified as to why he had been stripped of his uniform and all personal belongings.

Driving along behind the troop carrier was a battered jeep, the very one the lieutenant had been in with two companions at the time of his capture. We moved on through the pitch dark night, south to Wadi El Taqa and into the Quattara depression. There I transferred alone into the jeep, and my escort left me, with arrangements to meet me there in exactly 24 hours. I carried on east for about 20 miles, until I reckoned on being behind enemy lines, then swung north towards Wadi el Regel and the El Alamein area. Dawn broke, and in no time, quickly as it does in the desert, the sun appeared, giving perfect visibility to a small British observation plane above me. I stopped the jeep, stood up and waved, pointing to the north. The pilot came down low and circled, seemed satisfied at what he saw, gave me a wave and flew on. After a few more miles I slowed down when I saw a group of armoured vehicles on the horizon, and I approached them slowly, yelling in English and waving as hard as I could. The vehicles were manned by French troops; their officer spoke English, so I told him my story – lost on patrol, my companion killed, and I was trying to rejoin the 13th Corps. He didn't know anything about the 13th, said the officer, but the 44th was deployed about 10 miles further north, so maybe they could help. I drove on in the same direction, and passed behind row after row of all sorts of artillery ranged beside heaps of shells. I took note of the hundreds of tanks deployed at intervals and then eventually I was waved down and stopped by a sergeant in one of the groups. I repeated my story. The 13th is about 10 miles north, he said, but step down and have

some tea. You look done in so get some sleep and you'll be in time for the big show tomorrow. I had some biscuits and bully beef, washed them down with drinks of tea, and slept fitfully until late afternoon. Thanking the sergeant for his hospitality I drove off north, but as soon as the group were out of sight I swung south, grateful for the rapidly falling darkness. I had seen enough. Masses of artillery, groups of tanks and armour everywhere, and the talk of 'a big show' tomorrow. I reached the Quattara at about 9pm, and as I turned west towards my pick-up point the bombardment started. I had never seen or heard such a sight. The northern sky was bright with the muzzle flashes of big guns, and the swell of noise made it sound as though all the thunder in Africa had been unleashed above me. I had read in my history books about the massed artillery bombardments on the Western Front during World War I, and I thought to myself that this is what it must have been like. The guns went on without interruption for hours, then as the sun began to come up there was a sudden silence. My pick-up party had not appeared, and for the first time I began to feel the taste of fear in my mouth. I drove on through the silence for some miles, then turned north towards the wadi where the Folgore division, my starting off point, had been deployed. There was a terrible sight there. The ground was strewn with dead bodies and burnt-out armour and lorries. Smoke and the smell of burnt cordite hung over everything and not a living soul was to be seen. The ground was criss-crossed with the tracks of many vehicles and you could hear the moans of wounded men from amongst the wreckage. Some soldiers in British uniform lay among the heaps of dead. I thought hard. God alone only knew where my unit was, if now it existed at all. I could hear no sound of gunfire: I knew how fast advances and retreats could be in the desert; my comrades, if alive, could be scores of miles away. If

I were found here in a British uniform I was as good as dead,
for my deception would eventually come to light and I would
be executed as a spy.

I thought furiously. I started to search, and found a
dead Italian of more or less my size. Half his head had been
torn away by shrapnel, but apart from some bloodstains his
uniform was not too badly damaged. I stripped off my British
uniform and put on the dead man's, trying to quell my
revulsion at having to strip the almost headless remains of
what only some time ago had been a living human being. I
heaved his body up into my jeep, covered the body with
Lieutenant Martin's uniform and drove off half a mile or so
into the sand dunes and there buried the body and uniform as
best I could. I started to walk back towards the scene of the
battle, and on the way I buried my British identity tag and
papers and put on the tag of my dead Italian soldier. My name
was now Andrea Rotella, and I came from Cassino. Back
amongst the ruined vehicles and dead bodies, I took a deep
breath, cut my temple with a piece of shrapnel until blood
flowed, and began to hit my head as hard as I could against the
side of a ruined tank until I almost knocked myself out. I sat
there for a while then I crawled to join a little group of 10 or
so badly wounded Italians who had gathered about 50 yards
away, and was eventually picked up by a British burial patrol.
They took us to a dressing station, then on to a transit camp
in Egypt, then on to the camp on the Gareloch in Scotland
where I met you. On my return to Italy there was such a
shambles after the war that my new identity was never
questioned. I was demobbed as Andrea Rotella and made my
way back to Udine. The town centre had been bombed flat,
but luckily my home had not been touched, my parents were
still alive and after a while I was able to get my true identity
sorted out. And you know the rest, Mario.'

Mario leaned back, transfixed by the story.

'Amazing, amazing', he breathed. 'Would you like another coffee, Toni?'

Toni settled permanently in Scotland, prospered, and he and Betty had two more children. The two families, Mario's and his, grew up in a close friendship. Both men married Scottish girls, and they had once been behind the same brand of barbed wire. Toni died when comparatively young, and his story, which was never again mentioned, and which his family knew nothing about, died with him.

CHAPTER 13

Sammy

Sammy Corti was a regular weekly visitor to The Savoy. Every Thursday, as regular as clockwork, he would appear there punctually at 5pm and enjoy a supper before proceeding for an evening's entertainment at either a cinema or theatre. At the end of the performance he would return for a late cup of coffee, have a chat for a few moments with Mario, then return to his home in the north part of the city, where he lived alone with his parents. His visits to The Savoy had never been viewed with suspicion, as had those of Fabio the hero of another story told here (*see chapter 5*), for his family was in a different kind of business. He and his father owned a prosperous ice cream cafe in another part of the city, so there could have been no ulterior motive in his visits to The Savoy, as might have been the case in Fabio's visits.

These visits had been going on for a very long time

since the early thirties, and had been interrupted only by the intervention of the war, during which time both he and Mario were forcibly otherwise occupied. Before the war his visits were broken only by a period of six weeks each year, three weeks in the summer and three more weeks in the early winter, periods in which he engaged in much more adventurous pursuits.

His parents had emigrated to Scotland from the Naples area in the early 1900s and although Sammy himself was born in Glasgow, he retained strong emotional attachments to the country of his parent's birth, and when still a boy found there a hero who brought some glamour and pride into his humdrum existence. Mussolini had come to power in Italy in 1922 when Sammy was about six years old and as an impressionable boy Sammy would listen to his father extolling the virtues of Il Duce, whom he saw as the saviour of Italy and of Europe from the dark forces of Bolshevism.

With the intention of reflecting the magnificence of the new Italy, in the early thirties the Italian Government purchased a grandiose building in Park Circus to house the Consulate in Glasgow, and named it the 'Casa D' Italia'. This soon became known as 'La Casa del Fascio', 'Fascio' being the word derived from the ancient Roman symbol of civic power carried by the Lictors of that city, an axe tied inside a bundle of rods, and which now in modern times had given rise to the word 'fascism'. The 'Casa' became a focal point for the Italian colony in Glasgow, at least for those of them sympathetic to the Fascist regime in their homeland, for there were many Italians abroad who did not see eye to eye with the new regime in Italy.

There the young Sammy learned of the 'Balilla'. This was an organisation for boys and youths modelled on the Boy Scout movement in Britain, but with a distinct difference. The

Balilla was purely military in concept: the boys wore smart black uniforms with a tasselled cap, trained with imitation guns and underwent a disciplined regime, all this in holiday camps set in some of the most beautiful parts of Italy. Apart from the quasi-military training, all kinds of sporting events and social activities were laid on, and were tinged with skilful Fascist propaganda well-calculated to indoctrinate youthful minds.

Sammy was encouraged by his father to take part in this new movement, and in the exciting environment of the Balilla camps the young boy found escape from the monotony of his work in the family cafe. Even though it meant extra work for him in the shop during his son's absence the proud father was happy to have his boy do something for Il Duce and the new Italy. Moreover, the Balilla paid all travel expenses for its recruits, so the visits to Italy were in effect free holidays. So for two periods each year Sammy left behind his humdrum Glasgow life and revelled in the stirring atmosphere of a Balilla camp. He would return bronzed and fit and bubbling over with enthusiasm about his experiences there, which were recounted with relish and embellishment to Mario during his weekly visits to The Savoy.

The latter would listen just a trifle enviously but also quite sceptically to these tales, for although they shared a common Italian heritage the family influence was very different in each case. Mario's father had been a Socialist in his youth, a political opinion strengthened by his experiences in the trenches of World War I, and the regime in Italy was anathema to him, so much so that no member of his family was allowed to set foot in 'La Casa del Fascio'. In those days no Italian son dared to go against his father's wishes, so Mario did not even bother to raise the possibility of visits to the 'Casa d'Italia' or of a free holiday to a Balilla camp, knowing full well the outburst that would be provoked by such a suggestion.

But as the years passed and as his father grew older, Sammy had to devote more and more time to the family cafe and as his Balilla visits became less regular, so his aversion to his work increased and he began to hate the necessity of standing behind a claustrophobic shop counter day after day, dishing out ice cream wafers and serving McCallums and Bovrils at the cafe tables. For a full year he endured the monotony of this existence until he could stand it no more. He persuaded his father to employ someone in his place and made off to Italy for an extended period with the Balillas.

This was in 1936, just as civil war was about to erupt in Spain, a conflict which was to polarise political opinion in the rest of Europe, as Communist Russia sided with the Republican Government of Spain, and Germany and Italy supported the Franco rebels. This support soon took the form of material intervention in the war. Russia sent tanks, artillery, munitions and military advisers to the Republican side; Germany sent part of her Luftwaffe to assist Franco, and Mussolini, not to be outdone, decided to send two full divisions of Fascist volunteers to fight side by side with Franco's troops. The young Sammy was caught up in the storm of propaganda which swept through Italy. The radio and press blared that here was the Bolshevik enemy trying to establish a foothold in the Mediterranean; here was the opportunity for the glorious youth of Italy to fight for the noble cause of Fascism etc etc and Sammy, now about 20 years of age, was caught up in the national hysteria. In a burst of patriotic fervour, he found himself as a volunteer in the Italian Army sent to fight in Spain.

After a short period of training with real weapons in place of the imitations he had been used to in the Balilla, Sammy found himself on a troopship on its way to Valencia, a port under Franco's control, in the company of two divisions of young soldiers of his own age, all of them full of high

spirits and looking forward to the glamorous adventures to come.

Some time later, pinned down by enemy fire on the hills of Guadalajara, some 30 miles from Madrid, he came face to face with the reality of war. Here men were being killed in a variety of ghastly ways, bodies ripped open by bullets, limbs torn off by explosions, human beings with their brains and guts spilled open and troops freezing in the icy mud and sleet of a Spanish winter.

The irony of this battle being fought on Spanish soil was that the combatants were Italian on both sides. Facing the young Italian volunteers was the Garibaldi Division of Italian anti-Fascist expatriates, who were fighting against Franco and for their Socialist cause in the ranks of the famous International Brigade. These men were fighting for an ideal, and were battle hardened veterans who had no difficulty in routing their badly led and poorly motivated opponents. But Sammy was not a cowardly man, and during the headlong retreat of his companions he did not panic, and at considerable risk to himself, stayed behind to help his Captain, who had been badly wounded in the legs. He dragged him, under fire, to the comparative safety of a ruined farmhouse building, and during the cover of night Sammy carried the unconscious man on his back to their own unit, now re-grouped some miles back. The Fascist propaganda machine back in Rome had been churning out all sorts of mendacious accounts about imaginary victories against the Bolshevik armies in Spain, and here finally was a true event, a courageous action carried out by an ex-Balilla recruit, which could be used as a morale building true story to maintain enthusiasm for the intervention in the Spanish conflict.

Sammy was commended by his Colonel and returned as a conquering hero to Rome, where he was summoned by

the great Duce himself to be presented with a military decoration for his bravery in saving the life of a fellow soldier. Being only human, Sammy revelled in the adulation showered upon him, but his pleasure in all these events was tempered by the arrival of a letter from his father in Glasgow. His parent was not well, his mother too was ailing, and his presence was required back home to help carry on the family business. So after a few months, his exploit now forgotten by the Italian press, he was granted unlimited compassionate leave by the army, to find himself once more behind the cafe counter in Glasgow, with his desire for further adventure extinguished by the reality of his war experience in Spain.

Strangely enough, yet perhaps not so strangely, for in those days news reportage of an international nature was by no means comprehensive, not a single word of his exploits had percolated back to Glasgow. As a British subject born in Britain, Sammy was free to come and go as he pleased without check or hindrance by the authorities. As far as his acquaintances and customers were concerned, he had just been away for a couple of years for no apparent reason. Moreover at that time, because of the worsening international situation and with Mussolini sliding into his military pacts with Hitler, Sammy thought it prudent to keep the story of his military adventures in the Italian Army strictly to himself.

Two years passed. In 1939 Hitler invaded Poland, Britain and France declared war on Germany, and then in June 1940 Italy, not to be deprived of a share in what seemed to be a certain German victory, declared war on Britain. On that same day Sammy, as the British subject that he was, received calling up papers from the British Army, and was ordered to report to Maryhill barracks to begin his military service. Sammy had no desire whatsoever to serve in any army. His experiences on the cold Guadalajara plateau had cured him of

his desire to play soldier, and he did not relish the possibility of fighting against the very comrades he had served with not so long ago.

He thought long and hard about his situation, and was still thinking as he stood at attention in front of a choleric little Major in a room at the barracks. He waited as the officer consulted some papers.

'Now, Corti, I see here that your parents were born in Italy?'

'Yes sir,' answered Sammy, hesitantly.

'Do you speak Italian?' Conveniently forgetting that he was equally at home in both languages Sammy pondered for a second .

'Just a wee bit sir.'

'You know that Italy is now at war with us, so I'll have to get some background before I can find a post for you. Can you drive a car? Were you ever in the Boy Scouts? Were you ever in the Cubs? Have you any special ability?'

Sammy cleared his throat nervously.

'No sir, I've never been in the Scouts, but I served for nearly two years in the Littorio division of the Italian Army under General Roatta, and fought in the battle of Guadalajara in Spain.' He gave a small cough. 'And I was decorated by Mussolini with the Silver Military Cross for bravery in action.'

He spread out his Italian military papers in front of the speechless Major, topped them off with a glossy photograph of a beaming Duce in the act of pinning a decoration on his chest, and leaned back to await reactions.

They were not long in coming. A flabbergasted Major pawed feverishly through the papers, and stopped to stare for several seconds at the photo of Sammy standing stiffly to attention in front of his Duce. His face changed through several different colours,and finally settled into a vivid puce.

He let out a roar.

'Sergeant,' he yelled twice, and when the startled NCO appeared at the double he spluttered, 'Take this man and lock him up in the cells.'

And there Sammy languished for nearly a week. A battery of Intelligence Officers questioned him intensively about his Balilla activities and his military service in Spain. Through it all he felt quite badly done by. What had he done after all? Britain wasn't at war with Italy during his period of military service, so what was everyone on about? The questions exhausted, Sammy was interned under Wartime Regulation 18B, a law that allowed of the imprisonment of any person, irrespective of country of origin, who was deemed to be of danger to the State. Thus he remained for the best part of a year until released as a volunteer to serve in the Home Pioneer Corps, a branch of the army composed of every type of misfit who had ever donned a uniform, and whose work it was to clear the rubble from the bombed cities of Britain. That, reasoned Sammy, was better than vegetating behind barbed wire for the duration of the war, to be faced afterwards with a very uncertain future. After all, the family cafe was there to go back to afterwards and his customers would not be able to point the finger of scorn at him for not having served his country of birth during the war.

The war ended and Sammy returned to his post behind the counter of the café with his wild oats sown and his adolescent desire for adventure satisfied. On one of the walls of the shop there hangs a photo of himself as a sergeant in the British Army, the rank attained during his service in the Pioneer Corps.

Prominently displayed in the privacy of his home there is a framed photographic enlargement of his day of glory in Rome.

CHAPTER 14

Father Gilbert

*T*uesday evenings were a special occasion in the church hall of St Aloysius in Hill Street. In the winter months these were the evenings when Father Gilbert gave his lectures to the parishioners and to anyone else who cared to attend. These lectures were on a very high theological plane, and not surprisingly so, for Father Gilbert was a graduate of King's College, Cambridge where in his youth many years before, he had obtained a PhD in Divinity and History. The combination of the two subjects had taken him to the conclusion that the only possible way to preach and practise Christianity was to follow the way of Rome, and so, after years of deliberation he converted to Catholicism and became a Franciscan friar. After ordination his orders had taken him to several friaries in England until his appointment to his present post in the tiny Franciscan Friary on the banks of the Clyde at Uddingston.

There he had become renowned for the eloquence and power of his sermons, and so had been invited by the Jesuits to give a series of lectures at their church in Hill Street. This arrangement suited Father Gilbert admirably, for it gave him an opportunity to visit Glasgow city centre each week even if only for a short time, where he could enjoy the bustle and brightness so foreign to his Friary. Moreover, there was another incentive. There is nothing in the philosophy of St Francis that says that the flesh must always be mortified, and Father Gilbert had discovered the delights of Mario's fish teas in The Savoy, only a short distance away from St Aloysius on the road to the bus stop at Killermont Street bus station.

So he made a point of stopping off on the way each evening after his lectures for a quick meal there, and it was thus that he became acquainted with Mario. The young owner had ever a pleasant word to say to the priest who by now had become a regular customer, and when the reason for the father's visits to the area became known to him he too made a point of going to listen to the priest's discourses. Mario had a wide range of interests, was a voracious reader, and would enjoy nothing more than to listen and then discuss the various points of philosophy raised by Father Gilbert's sermons. For he had another cleric with whom he enjoyed discussion.

The Reverend Leslie Hope was the minister of the Renfield Street Church which stood at the top of Renfield Street at the corner of Sauchiehall Street. The Reverend was a member of the Western Baths club in Cranworth Street in Hillhead, as was Mario, and the two would sit in the cooling room of that august establishment to exchange views on matters in general and indulge occasionally in intense theological argument. The reason why they sat always in the cool room of the baths and not in any of the other steam or dry heat areas was because the Reverend had a condition

which rendered him unable to perspire, and excessive heat was not only uncomfortable but positively dangerous for him. Naturally Mario was a Catholic and, although a far from pious one, he was always ready to argue his corner in any discussion about religion. Mario's fervour, however, was no match for the erudition of the Reverend Leslie Hope, who had graduated with a PhD in Divinity at Edinburgh University, so Mario repeated the minister's arguments to an interested Father Gilbert, who supplied him with rebuttals and ammunition for further discussion with the Protestant Reverend. As a result, the two men of the cloth became known to each other through the medium of Mario, who longed for an opportunity to bring the two together and listen to them debate the issues which separated them.

This was not an easy matter. There was no such thing as an Ecumenical movement in those days. Protestants were still looked upon as heretics by the Catholic clergy and contact with them kept to a minimum. Equally Protestants regarded Catholics as papist idolaters and followers of the scarlet harlot of Rome. There was little or no contact between the relative ministers of the religions. Fraternisation might have been looked upon as an act of heretical treason.

Mario went about it cautiously, sounding out the opinions of the two, and to his delight found that the reverends would only be too pleased to meet face to face in order to continue the debates which they had been pursuing through Mario as a third party. So they were invited to Mario's home for dinner one evening, and replete with an excellent meal prepared by Mary his wife and mellowed by the accompanying wine, the two embarked on a fascinating evening's conversation. Another dinner was arranged and the meetings became a monthly occurrence. The two reverends looked forward to an evening in one another's company, and

Mario sat enthralled through the conversation that always ensued. Their talk was scintillating. They were both erudite and intelligent men who delighted in the cut and thrust of quick debate, and it became obvious that very little indeed separated them in the fundamentals of their relative religions. They became fast friends, although their meetings became less frequent as a result of the Reverend Hope's declining health. His by now rare visits to the baths stopped altogether and no one was surprised to hear that one night he had passed away peacefully in his bed. His will contained a hand-written request.

The morning of the funeral arrived and the Renfield Street Church filled to overflowing with mourners come to pay their last respects to a friend and valued member of the Church of Scotland. Close by the principal mourners stood the imposing figure of a man dressed in a plain brown flowing habit with a white cord round the waist. He wore sandals on his bare feet, and the cowl of his uniform was pulled back to reveal the carefully shaped tonsure on the crown of the head. Father Gilbert had come to pay his respects at the funeral in the manner desired by his dead friend.

Not so very long ago Father Gilbert himself passed away. He lies buried on the banks of the Clyde in a tiny cemetery close by his beloved Friary.

CHAPTER 15

Benny

*J*ohnny McMillan's gym was in Sauchiehall Street, between what used to be The Regal Cinema and Dalhousie Street, and in the middle thirties it was a Mecca for any who liked to rub shoulders with the boxing greats of that era. Boxing then was a very popular sport and still carried the name of 'the noble art of self defence'. Those were hard times and they produced hard people, and boxing offered a chance to anyone with the necessary physical attributes to escape from the grinding monotony and poverty of the slums of the cities. Names like Elky Clark, Tommy Milligan, Johnny McMillan, Sandy McKenzie, Johnny McManus, and Jim Campbell were known in every household in the land. Scotland had more than its share of great boxers in those days, and none were greater than Glasgow's own Benny Lynch, who in 1935 rose to international fame when he beat Jackie Brown of Manchester

119

to become world flyweight champion.

One of the attractions of Johnny McMillan's gym was the fact that Benny Lynch could be seen there almost every day, sometimes training, sometimes just lounging and basking in the adulation of his many hangers-on and admirers, the same ones who were just beginning to help him on to the slippery slope to alcoholism and oblivion.

The gym was just around from The Savoy, and Mario now spent some hours in the winter afternoons there with the bar-bells. and weights. He was on nodding acquaintance with Sammy Wilson, the bookie who had taken Benny under his wing, and who spent the occasional hour in the gym with his protégé. Wilson was a good customer in The Savoy. On a day when the gym happened to be much quieter than usual Mario was going through his weights routine watched by Sammy. The bookie divided his attention between Mario and his protégé Benny, who was shadow-boxing in the ring alone.

'Hello there Mario, how about giving Benny a couple of rounds? You've got the build for it.'

'No way,' replied Mario. 'I can't box.'

'Aw come on, just spar around for a few rounds, Benny won't hurt you. Just throw a few punches at him to give him some practise.'

Mario thought for a moment. He was far short of the quickness of movement boxing required, but weighed a good two and a half stones more than Benny and was as strong as a bull. The champion was a skinny eight stones, with an undernourished appearance that belied his fearsome reputation. What the hell, why not? Sammy Wilson helped him on with a well padded pair of gloves and shoved him into the ring.

They sparred around for a few minutes, Benny weaving in and out, throwing light punches at his sparring partner, urging him to try a few punches. Mario began to

enjoy the experience, relaxed, tried to copy his opponent's weaving and tried to land some punches of his own. Benny fell into a clinch, they wrestled about a bit and as they broke Mario hit him as hard as he could with a punch to the chest. The blow knocked Benny off his feet, but he regained his feet as quick as a flash and proceeded to annihilate the hapless Mario with a flurry of lightning fast blows to the head and body. Mario did his best to protect himself, but to no avail. The speed and ferocity of his skinny opponent was unstoppable, and he was saved from serious injury only by the immediate intervention of Sammy, who had leapt into the ring immediately to pacify his enraged boxer. Benny at once calmed down and patted the dazed Mario affectionately on the back of the head.

'Sorry about that. Ah lost the heid fur a minit. Ye shouldnay a hit me so hard. Ye made me lose the place,' and proceeded to wipe the blood from Mario's nose with a sweaty towel. Mario did not regain his good looks for a week, the time it took for his two black eyes to regain their natural colour and for his nose, fortunately unbroken, to regain its natural shape. He continued with his visits to the gym, but from that day on he stuck rigidly to his weight lifting routine.

The years passed, and Benny's life continued on its tragic path. He drank to excess and found it ever harder to make the weight and get into condition for his fights. He squandered his money and became a punching bag for opponents who five years before he could have beaten with one hand tied behind his back. In 1938, he was matched with a Rumanian, Aurel Toma. He went into the ring overweight, drink-sodden and unfit, and was knocked out in the fifth round. He was never to fight again.

The war intervened. In 1940, Mario was interned as an Italian POW and five years later returned to take up his

work in the family shop. A favourite item on The Savoy menu for late night drunken diners was tripe suppers, eaten by them in the belief that it helped the sobering up process.

Occasionally late at night the drunken figure of a man would reel into the shop, go unsteadily to a table and order up a tripe supper. The man would gulp it down quickly, then sit apathetically with glazed eyes looking blankly at the wall in front until closing time. He spoke to no one and bothered no one. At closing time Mario would go up to him with a pat on the back,

'It's closing time, Benny' then help him to his feet and guide him to the door, leaving him outside propped up against a wall. Those were always the only words spoken, and Mario would wonder if the memory of their brief encounter in Johnny McMillan's gym one day in 1935 lay dormant somewhere in Benny Lynch's drink-sodden brain. One night in August 1946 Benny seemed to be more comatose than ever when escorted to the door of The Savoy. Two days later Mario read in the evening paper that Benny Lynch had died in the Southern General Hospital of pneumonia.

CHAPTER 16

The House-breaker

*I*n the late forties and early fifties the slim and deferential Hugh Macintosh, better known simply as Tosh, was well-known in the Cowcaddens. Always quiet, unobtrusive and soft-spoken, he drank alone in the pub of his choice, Doherty's Bar at the top of Hope Street, just round the corner from his tenement house in Maitland Street, where he lived with his wife Betty and family of six. Betty was a proud and capable housewife and mother. Her three room and kitchen flat was always immaculately clean and tidy, which was no mean feat, since it housed eight adults. The outside toilet, shared by the household opposite on the landing, was kept as clean as a whistle, and always provided with an adequate supply of newspaper squares for personal use. Her qualities as a housewife were reflected in the rearing of her children. They were always neatly and cleanly dressed and were made to

attend school regularly under pain of a good thrashing if any 'plunking' were to take place. She was a devout churchgoer and insisted that all the family attend mass together on Sundays, including Tosh when at home, since his line of work often took him away from his family for longish periods. On these occasions he sat somewhat sheepishly by his family, avoiding eye contact with the officiating priest.

For Tosh was a house-breaker by profession, and if success in that field is to be judged by the number of burglaries carried out without arrest, then he was not a very good one, for he seemed to spend more time behind bars in Barlinnie than he spent at liberty .

He had drifted into his profession as a matter of course. As a boy in his early teens he had served his apprenticeship amongst the crowds of young boys who exuberantly roamed the streets of the Cowcaddens, pilfering anything they could get their hands on, apples and biscuits from the local greengrocer's, lumps of coal from a passing cart, penny coins left on a shop counter as change awaiting collection, or a purse momentarily left unattended by a careless shopper. They stole anything of any value at all that came their way in fact, providing it was small enough and light enough not to impede a hurried escape. When he reached the school leaving age of 14 Tosh had a number of unskilled jobs and came to the conclusion that if he were prepared to accept the risk of arrest and the occasional jail sentence he could earn infinitely more by stealing than he could in an honest job of work, and in much less time. So in his late teens he took to house-breaking. He was not a violent man and avoided all contact with the persons whose belongings he was stealing and did as little damage as possible to their houses. His distinctive modus operandi, however, soon became known to the police, and whenever a tidy house-

breaking job without any collateral damage was reported, then Tosh was the obvious suspect. By the time he was 20 Tosh had already been to jail several times. The rough company he found there did not alter his behaviour or appearance. During his periods of freedom he was always well dressed, impeccable in his manners and kind to the old folk, all of which made him much liked in his immediate neighbourhood in Maitland Street. Plus he never stole from his neighbours.

His well-groomed and polite manner drew to him the notice and affection of Betty, a neighbour from one of the nearby streets. She was a pretty girl, from a devout churchgoing family who without success did all they could to discourage the relationship and soon, after a short courtship, the two were married. For some time Tosh kept to the straight and narrow. With the help of the local priest and with the urging of his new wife, he found a reasonably well paid job as a timekeeper in the nearby Buchanan Street goods station, but after some time, lured by the temptation of some easy money, he reverted to his old ways. A series of house-breakings in the Bearsden area brought him again to the attention of the police. These encounters with the law resulted in renewed visits to his old lodgings in Barlinnie, and it was there that he met Lino Valle, the notorious Scots-Maltese safecracker.

It was said of Lino that, given enough time, he could open any safe ever made, and his skills had been put to the test by the British Intelligence services during the recent war. MI5 had reason to believe that a safe in the German Embassy in neutral Lisbon contained highly sensitive military codes. They itched to get a sight of these documents, but did not dare take any overt illegal action to get their hands on them. It was an unwritten convention between the warring powers and their neutral Portuguese hosts that no government should stoop to illegal practises in neutral territory in the furtherance of their

interests, so this ruled out the direct blunderbuss approach of a robbery. Plus the fact that stealing the safe would have also alerted the Germans to the loss of valuable documents. Subtler and more covert tactics were required. At this time Lino Valle was in prison for safe-breaking, for although he was the best there was in that art, his methods too were well-known to the police and rendered him prone to arrest. No mess, no violence, just straight in and out, open the safe, take whatever was of value, and away.

Lino was serving a longish sentence, so he grabbed the offer made to him by the authorities with both hands. All he had to do was to open a safe in a certain foreign country and close it again after the documents in it had been photographed. That was it, nothing else. The preparations, entry to the premises, transportation, etc. would be laid on. In exchange he would be given a pardon and a sum of money to help him cope in his new found liberty. Not only was the slate being wiped clean, but Lino was doing his patriotic duty in helping his native land keep the hated Italians and Germans at bay.

So the exploit was carried out. Lino was flown to Portugal and one dark night a bribed servant of the Embassy opened the door to a team of British agents equipped with the very best in photographic equipment. Lino opened the safe in record time, the contents were photographed, the safe closed, and the burglars departed, leaving not a trace of their visit. The affair produced invaluable information for the British and Lino was immediately released with a handsome gratuity and his fulsome promises that he would henceforth mend his ways.

But in the last months of the war the lure of easy money proved too hard to resist. A trail of opened safes led once again to Lino Valle and he found himself once more behind bars, this time sharing a cell with Tosh, who had

yielded to temptation in the stealing of some cash from an unattended office. The two got on well together. They were both quiet and well-behaved, kept clear of the hard cases who abounded in Barlinnie and finished their respective sentences on the same day. The friendship carried on into civvie street, and although Lino lived on the far side of town he visited his new friend at his home in the Cowcaddens from time to time. Betty made no objection to these visits. Tosh's new friend was quiet, polite and well-spoken. She quite liked him and although she knew nothing at all about him apart from the fact that he was a foreigner, she quite happily put out her best teapot and laid out her finest table for his visits.

At the corner of Maitland Street, and the Cowcaddens, in the tenement block adjacent to the one where Tosh and Betty lived, Freddie, the local Tally, had his cafe. This establishment was famous in the district. Teresa, Freddie's wife, came from a region in Italy near Naples, and had brought with her to Glasgow the formula for a perfect ice cream. Just before the outbreak of war they had set up their little cafe and had made their home on the top storey above it. They proceeded to sell the best ice cream in all of Glasgow and customers came from afar to try it. The little business flourished and prospered. But then war clouds loomed and Freddie, born in Glasgow, was called up to do his military service in the British Army. With the outbreak of war and the introduction of food rationing, Teresa was left alone to run the business. She found it impossible to obtain the ingredients for her ice cream and could barely earn enough to pay the rent with the sale of cigarettes, which were also in short supply, and the meagre supply of sweets and bars of chocolate allocated to her for sale in the little shop. But not for long. When there are shortages and rationing, ways will always be found to circumvent regulations and Teresa began to obtain a

weekly supply of a few gallons of black market milk from a local farmer. With this and a few pounds of illicitly obtained sugar she could make several gallons of her delicious ice cream, and could sell it in the course of a few hours, summer or winter, to her customers, who had been for so long starved of delicacies and sweet things. Incredible but true, this illegal sale of ice cream never came to the attention of the local food office and lasted for the duration of strict food rationing, a period of more than five years, and had amassed for Teresa a considerable amount of cash. The sum of £8,000 lay neatly stacked in notes in a large old fashioned safe which she kept in the corner of her parlour, covered and hidden by an intricately knitted tapestry. On his occasional leaves from the army Freddie would help in the counting of all this largesse and gave fervent thanks for his luck in having found such an enterprising and devoted wife. They whispered to one another for hours in bed at night, conjuring up plans for the use of all this lovely money once Freddie was out of uniform and back in civvie street.

For health reasons Tosh had been rejected for military service and had served out the war doing a series of jobs in the district until his latest fall from grace which had earned him some months in the cell as a companion to Lino. For several years he had been a regular customer of Freddie's cafe, buying all his cigarettes there, and bringing home a pile of ice cream wafers to Betty and the children on the days when Teresa had ice cream for sale. The flow of cash into the register on these occasions did not escape his notice and his lips drooled not only at the lovely taste of ice cream but at the thought of how much money must be hidden away. It must be planked someplace, he reasoned. It came from black market sources and therefore could not be put into a bank where awkward questions might be asked. He began to think about breaking

into Teresa's flat to reconnoitre, but the years of self-discipline in not soiling his own doorstep deterred him for a while. Temptation however was too great. Teresa and Freddie were Tallys, so they didn't really count as neighbours, so one day when Teresa was busy in the shop doling out her black market ice cream, Tosh shinned up the rone pipe at the back of the tenement, carefully levered open the window, and taking the greatest of care, thoroughly searched the flat. The hiding place for the cash was obvious: the massive safe covered by a coloured cloth, but it presented an insurmountable obstacle for Tosh. He was a house-breaker, not a safe-breaker, so he retreated disconsolately down the rone pipe, leaving not the slightest indication that an intruder had been in the flat. The image of that safe haunted him for months, but the haunting ceased when he found himself in the same cell as Lino. They were both lone operators by nature, but their characters were so similar that when Tosh finally found the courage to broach the subject, Lino eagerly agreed to supply the expertise in the opening of the safe. One day when Teresa was busily engaged in dishing out wafers, Tosh climbed up the rone pipe, and opened the front door for his friend who in half a minute had expertly opened the forbidding-looking but ancient safe. Almost gibbering with delight they took note of the cornucopia of banknotes neatly piled inside, and proceeded to pack the money into two bags brought along for the purpose. An exchange of experiences had made them realise that a change of behaviour was necessary to throw the police off the track. The flat was turned upside down and the lock of the safe damaged with a heavy hammer blow to give the impression of a forced entry, and the two robbers left, laden down with their newly acquired fortune.

Poor Teresa. Her shock at finding the ransacked flat and empty safe can well be imagined. The police were called,

the place examined, but there was no clue as to who the perpetrator or perpetrators might have been. Teresa could make no mention of the large sum of money in the safe, as tricky questions might be asked, so an infinitely smaller sum was reported as stolen and she was left to pour out her grief in a long letter to her soldier husband. But youth is resilient, Freddie was soon demobbed and back in the cafe at work, and since there was nothing else for it, the loss of all that hard earned money was put to the back of their minds. They continued where they had left off at the beginning of the war, with no money, but with good health and plenty of time to make another fortune, this time more or less legitimately.

As for Tosh, he too began a new life. The money was split straight down the middle, with £4,000 each. This was a colossal windfall, and somehow had to be put into legitimate circulation. Nothing is known as to the fate of Lino's share, but Tosh, guided by Betty, made good use of his shadier Cowcaddens acquaintances. There was many a semi-honest bookie who would gladly take £4,000 in cash, no questions asked, and give back a cheque for £3,000, to be explained as a series of lucky results by the punter, and this last sum was ceremoniously deposited in the bank by Tosh and Mary. Good use was made of it. A sizeable bungalow could be bought in one of the Glasgow suburbs for less than £1,000 then, and this having been done, a proportion of the rest bought Betty and Tosh a nice little newsagent's business which kept them in middle class gentility for the rest of their lives.

CHAPTER 17

Betty

Renfrew Street runs from the site of the present Royal Concert Hall, from what used to be Killermont Street, directly west until it joins St Georges Road at Charing Cross. Its path is crossed by Cambridge Street and here the Cowcaddens district ends and the Garnethill area begins. In the fifties Garnethill was almost exclusively made up of large detached houses and superior quality tenements, dominated architecturally by St Aloysius church in Rose Street and Charles Rennie Mackintosh's School of Art building in Renfrew Street a few yards away. The area had few shops of any consequence and so the inhabitants had to do most of their shopping in the Cambridge Street area, which to all intents and purposes was part of the Cowcaddens district. The large houses of Garnethill, built at the end of the 19th Century for the use of the rich merchants of the city, were by now almost all used as

small bed and breakfast hotels and lodging houses, much sought after by travelling salesmen and by the scores of music hall artistes who appeared weekly at the City Centre theatres. The tenements were inhabited by 'respectable' working class families who considered themselves a cut above the rougher and somewhat less fastidious inhabitants of the tenements in the Cowcaddens proper.

One such was the Anderson family who lived in a neat and welltended flat in a tenement at 43 Buccleuch Street, in the shadow of St Aloysius, their parish church. The jewel of the Anderson household was their little daughter Betty, a friendly and vivacious pretty girl of four years of age. The child was well-known to everyone in the district as she played with her companions in the street and accompanied her mother on shopping trips to the local shops, 'going for the messages'. As a special Saturday treat from her fourth birthday onwards a visit to the 'pictures', was always laid on by her parents, which consisted of a matinee visit to a cartoon or children's film at one of the many cinemas in Cowcaddens. There was hardly a cinema usherette or shop assistant who did not know wee Betty Anderson.

The little girl was not due to start school until the age of five but already at the age of four and a half she attended a nursery close by in New City Road about five minutes walk away from her home. She was taken there by her parents on four mornings each week and collected either by them or by one of the neighbours at midday, at which time, after a midday 'piece', she would go off to play happily with other children of the district. Tenement backyards and street pavements served the children as a playground.

There was then little local crime as we know it nowadays in Glasgow. No car theft, for very few had a car, no vandalism, for each little tenement community was closely

knit and anyone with anti-social tendencies would immediately be disciplined by parents or neighbours, and, most important of all, by the 'polis' on the beat, who would administer a summary cuffing to any youth found in transgression of the law. Indeed many a parent would call on the help of the man on the beat to discipline an unruly child, and the police would often be asked to carry out a punishment which should rightly have been applied by the parents themselves. Child molestation must certainly have existed: it seems hardly likely that such activity could be just a modern occurrence, but if it did no publicity was given to it, and parents thought it perfectly safe to allow their children to play in the streets and backyards unsupervised.

So the Andersons thought nothing of allowing little Betty to roam around alone to play with her friends, as her shouted name would always suffice to bring her home when required. No one thought of the Garnethill area and the neighbouring Cowcaddens as being unsafe for children until the night that little Betty disappeared .

It was the night of 7 October 1952. The weather had been good in Glasgow that summer, the warm sunny days had carried over into the beginning of autumn and the children were allowed to play outside well into the onset of dusk. Betty's mother had prepared the evening meal and went into the close to call in her daughter, whom she had seen playing in the backyard some minutes before. She shouted several times, but no Betty appeared. As the minutes ticked by with no response to her cries a cold and gnawing worry began to take hold and she set off in search of her daughter, shouting her name at the top of her voice. She banged on the doors of neighbouring houses. All the other children were already inside, but there was no sign of her little Betty and no-one had seen her during the last half hour.

The police were hurriedly called and an immediate search of all the backyards and closes in the area was started. Darkness had by now set in and beams of light from police torches criss-crossed the night as they hurried from close to close and backyard to backyard, incessantly shouting the girl's name, hoping against hope for an answer. No trace of the little girl could be found. The search carried on through the night. Neighbours joined in the search, every backyard, every midden, every possible hiding place was searched, but to no avail. Little Betty Anderson had simply vanished from the face of the earth.

Next morning the biggest search ever mounted by the Glasgow police began. The head of the northern division CID, Neil Beaton, put every available man out on the streets to search for the little girl. Detective Superintendent Robert Calhoun brought in extra men from outlying divisions to assist and literally hundreds of neighbours joined in the search. Someone reported having seen the little girl in the company of a man in a department store, Trerons in Sauchiehall Street on the day of her disappearance. The shop was closed and searched from top to bottom by scores of police and firemen, but to no avail. Finally, on 9 October, two days after her disappearance, the dead body of the missing girl was discovered hidden in a backyard in Buccleuch Lane.

The whole of Glasgow seethed with anger and revulsion at the crime. Scores of beat men and as many plain clothes CID officers combed the area for clues. Every shop, every workplace and every household within a quarter mile radius of Betty's home was visited by the police and the occupants closely questioned, but no one could give the police the slightest indication as to who the murderer of Betty might be. A total of 1,500 men of the district were fingerprinted in an attempt to match some smudged prints found near the

body. All sorts of rumours abounded: crowds in their
hundreds gathered at Maitland Street police station to await
news: every coming and going from the station was observed
and commented upon. Rumour followed on rumour. Crowds
stood for hours in front of Trerons. The place had been
searched, so something must have gone on there, it was
reasoned. The police were on the lookout for a plain brown
van seen in the street at the time of Betty's disappearance, it
was rumoured. Vigilantes stopped scores of vans in the streets
and had to be dispersed by the police. The dreadful crime had
given birth to something akin to mass hysteria in the
neighbourhood.

Suspicion for the crime centred on Tom, a withdrawn
recluse of peculiar habits who lived a stone's throw from the
Anderson household. He was a dirty and unkempt shambling
figure of a man who seldom spoke to anyone, and was the
butt of shouts and jeers by local children as he trudged along
the pavements pushing in front of him an old pram which he
used to carry his messages and belongings. There was
something in his demeanour and his evasive answers to
questions that aroused police suspicion, and he was taken back
and forth to the Maitland Street police station over the course
of some days and subjected to relentless questioning in an
attempt to break down his constant protestations of
innocence. He was stripped and searched and his body and
clothing meticulously examined. There was no direct evidence
that the recluse had had anything to do with Betty's murder;
forensic science was in its infancy in those days, and where
nowadays a simple DNA test might have resolved everything,
there was no evidence to justify the arrest of the old man on
the charge of murder.

Taking part in the investigation was a young
policeman, Joe Beattie, who had just resumed a police career

135

interrupted by the war. He had been recently demobbed from the RAF with a conspicuous war record as a Pathfinder pilot and was later to rise to the rank of Chief Detective Inspector in the Glasgow CID. He assisted in the questioning of old Tom for hours on end, and was later to admit that he could reach no conclusion as to the man's innocence or guilt. He just looked the part, that was all, and you cannot accuse a man of murder just because of his appearance.

In his retirement, Joe Beattie would often muse on the fact that his first murder case had ended in failure, as did his last some 25 years later, when as a senior CID officer he headed the investigations into the unsolved Bible John murders until forced to retire because of ill health.

The murder of Betty Anderson was never solved. Her death cast a dark shadow of fear on Garnethill and Cowcaddens, and for a time little groups of vigilantes stood by as their children played on the pavements and backyards of the area. Old Tom's comings and goings at the police station had been noted by the public. Everyone believed him guilty and after his interrogations he never returned to his home for fear of retribution. He was rumoured to have died in a model lodging house at Anderson Cross some months later.

CHAPTER 18

Big Emma

At the time of Italy's declaration of war on Britain in the June of 1940 Big Emma had long become somewhat of an institution and legend in the Cowcaddens. As one of the many Italians who emigrated to Scotland at the early part of the century, she had arrived in Glasgow from the Barga district in Tuscany in the year 1921, together with her husband and newly-born son, to seek fortune, or at the least, the living which was not to be had in their homeland. They were an oddly matched couple. He stood all of five feet four inches in height and skinny with it, whilst she towered 16 stones and eight inches above him, a veritable whale of a woman. She was the driving force in the family. Born in a peasant community 25 years before in the hills above Barga, she had listened as a girl to the stories told by her elders about the great world of opportunity that lay overseas and about the money and

137

comfort to be had in America and suchlike places for those willing to work. She dreamt that one day she too would leave behind the backbreaking and fruitless farm labour into which she had been born and go in search of a life of ease and comfort in distant lands.

She dreamt too about marriage, to a strong and virile man who would take her away from the poverty and the drudgery of her life and who would satisfy the hot desires which would at times be assuaged by furtive romps in a barn or haystack with lusty workers from neighbouring farms. She welcomed such escapades, despite the necessity and embarrassment of confessing the same sin to the parish priest each month. This was a mandatory visit, for the young girls of the village were expected to take communion on the first Sunday of each month, and who would risk eternal damnation by accepting the host unshriven, or the opprobrium of your fellow villagers by not attending Sunday Mass?

Her somewhat uninhibited behaviour had earned her a justified reputation among the eligible bachelors in the area, all of whom shied well clear of marriage with such an insatiable Amazon. As she turned into her twenties and approaching spintershood (for in such societies women married when only in their teens) she decided that she must at all costs find a husband who would confer upon her respectability and the prospect of emigration to another land. In those backward country areas it was the Church, with its international ramifications, that often acted as travel agent and labour recruit, and a parish priest tended always to favour emigration requests from married couples.

So she found a husband, Alfredo, a somewhat shy and retiring labourer from a neighbouring village who also wanted to emigrate somewhere and thus needed a wife. Alfredo did not mix much with people and was not aware of

the formidable reputation of his new _innamorata_. He was small and thin and not very virile in appearance, completely at variance in appearance with his tall, busty and lusty looking bride and in the process of marrying them the priest decided that he would do all he could to find work for them abroad. He had had enough of giving absolution to Big Emma for the sins of the flesh and had no desire to hear from her the adulterous transgressions which no doubt would result from such a union. Let another priest somewhere take up the burden.

In a place called Glasgow in the north of Britain a few Italian families from the Barga area had set down roots and had prospered, opening up fish and chip shops and cafes. These families now needed workers for their businesses: locals might have been available despite the long and unsociable hours of work, but employers were far more comfortable working with their own kind, so willing workers were sent for from the homeland. They had the same language and the same culture, and in the handling of cash they could to a certain extent be trusted: in a strange land and in an alien environment peer pressure in the form of losing face back home if a job were lost through dishonesty was enough to ensure good behaviour, for a while at least.

So one bleak and miserable February day Alfredo and his wife and their newly-born son arrived in the Cowcaddens, at the top of Maitland Street, to be precise, where Alfredo's employer had found lodgings for his new worker and his family. A starker contrast to their home village could hardly be imagined with its dark grey soot-stained tenements with closes dripping condensation. They were little better than slum dwellings, with a dull, heavy sky seeming to touch the chimney heads, and alien tongues and accents everywhere. Rough-looking men with flatcaps and scarves round their

necks, women in dark shawls, beer houses everywhere with drunks propped up against the walls. These were the scenes that confronted Alredo and Emma. But in those days emigrants from any land were made of stern stuff and Big Emma and Alfredo had more than their share of backbone. They had left home because they wanted to work and to save and to prosper, and so they did just that, learning the language as best they could, ignoring their environment and putting a few shillings aside each week so that a shop of their own could be acquired some day.

That day soon arrived, and a new fish and chip shop appeared on the scene, 'Emma's' at the Port Dundas end of the Cowcaddens. Given that a few pounds for the necessities were available, it was easy then to open up that type of business. No town planning to cope with, no troublesome sanitary regulations: just pick your spot, and for a chip shop all that was needed was a back shop to gut the fish and wash the potatoes, a large stove to fry them, some paper to wrap them in, a counter over which to serve them, and a capacity for hard work for 12 hours and more of the day. Emma and Alfredo prospered. Their shop was perfectly situated. Buchanan Street goods station was only a few yards away with its hundreds of porters and carters, Dobbies Loan with its scores of workshops lay behind them and they were surrounded by grimy tenements with hundreds of potential customers. Most important of all, the area was more than well provided with pubs and cheap drinking dens.

A cheap but limited menu was on offer. A bag of chips was a penny. A fish supper was fourpence, a pie supper was threepence and a black pudding supper was the same price. Plus there was the speciality of the house! Pig's feet and fritters for only fourpence! They did a roaring trade from morning till night. Emma had soon acquired a working knowledge of the

language and with a pronounced Italian accent could match the rough jargon and swearing of the locals with an invective all her own in her dealings with them. Her energies were taken up completely in the running of the shop and the counting of her shillings and she had no thought or time for anything else: the somewhat feeble night-time efforts of Alfredo aroused no further passion in her and the local priest had an easy time in coping with her monthly confession of very venial sins.

Then at the beginning of the thirties disaster struck. Alfredo took ill one winter's day and died, leaving Emma alone with their young boy and the busy shop. She grieved a little. Although she had grown genuinely fond of Alfredo, the marriage had been one of convenience for her and she had achieved her aim, to leave behind the grinding poverty of the Barga hills for another land. Never mind that the work in Glasgow was long and hard. Never mind that she had to put up with rough and uncouth customers, she was as rough and earthy as they were, if not more so. Never mind the dull tenements and the grey and cold winters. The pennies and the shillings were rolling in, and despite the death of her husband she now had another dream, a little piece of land on some gentle slope in Tuscany, with a little house and a few vines and perhaps a cow for fresh milk.

A worker to replace her dead husband arrived from Italy and she carried on alone in the running of the shop. If they had ever existed at all, marital constraints were now lifted, and Emma began to respond in kind to the many advances received from her customers. She liked big men and they were in plentiful supply in the district, from the workplaces around the shop to the local police station, where big men abounded, more than willing to console and service the buxom widow after a snack of pig's feet and fritters in the

back shop. And so the fame of Big Emma's chip shop grew, as did the little pile of money accumulating in the bank, until war broke out with Germany in the September of 1939, at which point business got even better. Soldiers of many nationalities filled the streets. Money flowed like water, the pubs did a roaring trade, and the queues at Emma's chip shop counter grew even longer.

Then in June of the following year the thread supporting the sword of Damocles hovering over the head of the Italian colony in Britain snapped. Mussolini declared war on Britain and the thousand or so Italians living in Scotland suddenly became enemy aliens, and that night few were the Italian shops which were not systematically destroyed and looted in the name of patriotism by gangs of marauding hooligans.

Big Emma was seated in her back shop at six o'clock that evening listening to the wireless when the programme was interrupted to give the news of Italy's entry into war. As she sat digesting the announcer's words she was aroused from her reverie by the sound of shouts in the street outside. There outside her shop swirled a crowd of drunken hooligans bent on destruction. Snatching up a heavy metal chip basket in a powerful hand she confronted the seething crowd and heard shouts of

'Mussolini, Mussolini, there's a Tally shop, do it in.'

She stretched to her full height and raised the chip basket, shook it at the crowd and roared in a thick Scots-Italian accent.

'Fuck Mussolini. Fuck Hitler. Fuck you all. Don't you touch anything, you bastards. You would all eat shite if I fried it!'

This magnificent non sequitur stopped the crowd dead in its tracks. A hush descended and a laugh at Emma's

words rippled through the mob. A shout rang out.

'Come on, we'll find some place else to do in. Ye canny touch her, she's a wumman.' And the mob drifted off in search of another Tally target.

For the rest of the war Emma kept her shop open and was never bothered or insulted again by her rough neighbours and customers because of her nationality. She did a record trade despite the lack of raw materials. Fish were often in short supply, but potatoes and pig's feet could be had in abundance from the black market sources which Emma soon became adept at finding, and her little pile of savings grew by the minute.

The war ended and the redevelopment of Glasgow began. Buchanan Street goods station closed down, the workshops in Dobbies Loan were demolished to make way for the eventual ring road around the city and the demolition of the Cowcaddens slums began. Emma's customers dwindled to practically nothing, and in the middle fifties she called it a day. The shop door was closed for the last time and she returned to her native Tuscany for the first time in 30 years, a relatively rich woman.

During those years she had never travelled outside of Glasgow. Her much dreamed of little piece of land in Tuscany was never acquired. She invested instead in a little seven room bed and breakfast hotel in Lerici, a beautifully picturesque fishing village south of Genoa much frequented by tourists from northern Europe. Scottish visitors are made especially welcome, and they come away amazed and somewhat bewildered by her fluent but somewhat fractured flow of Cowcaddens English, in which she claims that her 30 or so years in the Cowcaddens were the happiest of her life.

CHAPTER 19

The Stone

At the end of the year 1950 England and the Empire were suddenly thrown into turmoil. Treason seemed to be afoot. The shadow of a possible Scottish Guy Fawkes had fallen on the land and the establishment in Westminster began to go in fear of revolution and retribution. The names of William Wallace and Robert the Bruce were uttered in hushed tones in the corridors of power, and anyone with a Scottish accent was looked upon with suspicion. A mighty and unexpected blow had been delivered to the very seat of the English Monarchy. The Stone of Scone, the historic Stone of the Destiny of the Scottish people and the potent symbol of the authority of the English Crown over the long vanquished Scots had been stolen from beneath the coronation chair in Westminster Abbey. The stone, which, as myth had it, was once Jacob's pillow and had served as seat for the crowning of 110 Scottish kings over the

144

centuries, had been carried off to London by the conquering Edward 1 of England in 1296. There, in Westminster Abbey, it was placed under the coronation chair as a symbol of the subjugation of the Scots and over it, for 650 years English kings and queens were crowned, symbolically squatting over the very soul of the Scottish peoples.

On Christmas Eve 1950, the five hundredweight mass of stone had vanished without trace, leaving behind a few splinters of wood where it had been torn from its fastenings. Scotland exulted and chortled at the daring of the perpetrators. England was outraged at this effrontery to the nation and spoke of vulgar and unwarranted vandalism. Immediately Scotland Yard went into action and a massive investigation, centred naturally around Scottish Nationalists and dissidents north of the border, swung into action.

There is a school of philosophy which claims that if a butterfly were to flutter its wings in the Gobi desert the ripples of that action would eventually be felt thousands of miles away. If Mario Petri of the Cowcaddens Savoy had known of that particular theory, the manner in which the liberation of the Stone in Westminster was to touch his own life in the Cowcaddens some days later would have forced him to endorse it fully, and to explain this a digression is necessary.

At the time of these momentous events in London, Mario was in the process of re-integrating into Scottish society after having been classified as an enemy alien for the period of the war just recently ended. This classification had resulted in his internment and deportation to a camp in Canada. One of the conditions of his release back to Glasgow was that he should undertake 'work of national importance', and to fulfil this condition he had found work in a piggery on the outskirts of Glasgow owned by a certain Tam McSeveney. Much as he revelled in his new-found freedom in driving a brock wagon

around the streets of Glasgow he found it irksome that
because of his duties at the piggery he could devote no time
to the family business, The Savoy Restaurant, which his aged
parents had with difficulty kept going during the war years.
No doubt, eventually he could have obtained official
permission to return to his pre-war occupation, but hearsay
had it that such permits were a long time in coming. So Mario
decided to take a short-cut in the matter and one day
approached Tam, with whom he had become quite friendly.

'Look here, Tam. You're paying me 3 pounds 10 a
week, aren't you ?'

McSeveney looked at him suspiciously.

'Don't you be asking for a rise, because you're no
gettin' it.'

'No, no, I don't want a rise. Just to say that if you keep
stamping my books and letting on that I'm still working for
you, I'll give you 6 pounds 10 a week to let me attend to my
own business.'

The pig farmer looked at him, mind racing. '6 pounds
10,' he thought. 'I could pay another man 3 pounds 10 and I'd
be three quid in pocket.'

'Aye, well, maybe, but you'd have to look in at the
piggery now and then, just to make things look right.'

And so the deal was done. As far as the world in
general and the authorities in particular were concerned,
Mario was employed at the piggery, but in actual fact he was
devoting all his energies to the expansion of the family
business and was paying Tam McSeveney 6 pounds 10 each
week for the opportunity of doing so.

This expansion had taken the form of a new cafe, The
Silver Lounge, just a few yards away from The Savoy. The cafe
was built on two levels, on the ground floor were the service
counter and a dozen or so comfortably seated tables, and

upstairs was a large room with seating accommodation for a hundred or so customers. Apart from the quality of its coffee and ice cream, the main attraction of The Silver Lounge was the background music provided. Over the years Mario had collected hundreds of gramophone records, ranging from operatic arias by Gigli through the crooning of Bing Crosby to the jazz of Ellington and Armstrong. A list of these was placed on each table, and the customers could have their choice of music on request. These records were played on a turntable in the back shop and relayed through the premises by means of a single loudspeaker on the ground floor and two large speakers in the upstairs room.

During the summer months on Saturdays and Sundays the upstairs room was reserved exclusively for the use of a group of nature lovers and hill walkers who congregated there for their weekend meetings and discussions. They called themselves 'The Hikers', and the membership consisted almost exclusively of young Scottish Nationalists culled from all walks of life and mostly still wet behind the ears.

There was a fair share of eccentrics amongst them, not the least outlandish of whom was their leader, Wendy Wood, head of the Scottish Nationalist Party. Wendy Wood was a woman who had lived her life for the Scottish cause and who had done everything in her power to keep the flame of Scottish Nationalism alive during the years when other small matters, such as the defeat of Hitler, was keeping the nation otherwise occupied. In the immediate post-war years she had redoubled her efforts to have the Stone of Destiny returned to its rightful place, and to this end was frequently photographed in the Royal Mile in full Scottish regalia, sporting a sandwich board emblazoned with the words 'Where is the Stone of Destiny?'

She presided regally over the weekly cafe meetings of 'The Hikers', sweeping majestically into the premises, clad in

full tartan regalia, acknowledging with a wave of the hand the deference of her acolytes, who listened to her every word as if it was gospel. Eccentric she may well have been in her dress and in her actions, but she had a case to state and did it eloquently and efficiently.

Quite naturally, on the disappearance of the Stone of Destiny police investigations north of the border focussed on Wendy and her group, and one night just before closing time, a young CID constable, Joe Beattie, well known to Mario, came through the doors of The Silver Lounge.

'Hello Mario, can I have a wee word ?' and leading him by the elbow into a secluded corner, continued, 'Nothing to worry about, but when the shop's clear there's a couple of the big brass from the Central would like a word with you.'

Bells of warning had begun to tinkle in Mario's ear. Had his deception been uncovered? Did the authorities know that the only work of national importance he did at the piggery was the handing over of 6 pounds 10 each week to big Tam? What would the repercussions be if he had been found out? Big brass from the central division? Surely his deception did not warrant the use of such heavy artillery?

Mario worried, the cafe cleared, and Joe Beattie went out and returned two minutes later accompanied by two imposing looking figures dressed in mufti. Mario immediately recognised one of them, an occasional visitor to The Savoy, Detective Inspector Kerr. The inspector stepped forward and introduced his companion.

'Hello Mario. I want you to meet Mr Ferguson.'

The tinkling warning bells in Mario's head reached a crescendo.

'Mr Robert Ferguson?' he asked, and the knot in his stomach tightened at the affirmative nod. The name was notorious in the Italian colony as belonging to the official

who had so enthusiastically carried out Churchill's injunction to 'Collar the Lot' when asked what should be done about the Italians resident in Britain at the outbreak of war. So enthusiastically indeed had Ferguson carried out the order that it was joked that anyone who had ever eaten Italian ice cream was liable to be arrested and interrogated.

'Damn it, I've been rumbled,' thought Mario, 'I should have applied to the Home Office a long time ago,' and he tensed, waiting for the hammer to fall.

Ferguson's stone-like face cracked into the semblance of a smile.

'I hear good reports about you Mario. You've settled in well after your trip to Canada, I see,' referring to Mario's place of internment five years before. 'How did you get on there?'

'Fine, great, fine,' came the answer, masking the thought 'I wish he would stop buggering about and come straight to the point.'

'We'd like you to do us a favour.' continued Ferguson, looking around him at the arrangement of the cafe. 'I hear that Wendy Wood and her friends come here every weekend. Could I see where they meet?'

The knot in Mario's stomach began to ease. Maybe this wasn't about his irregularity after all, and as the detectives stood in the upstairs room and looked around, the bells in his head ceased to ring. 'Thank God, this isn't about me after all.' Ferguson looked around him asked for explanations about the two large loudspeakers on the wall.

'Excellent.' He rubbed his hands briskly. 'Excellent, couldn't be better.' He placed an avuncular hand on Mario's shoulder and proceeded to tell the relieved cafe owner what was expected of him, as a favour of course.

It was proposed that the two loudspeakers should be converted into microphones which would pick up

conversation in the room and relay it to a suitable point on the premises, where it would be monitored and recorded by a police officer. It only remained for a hidden monitoring place to be chosen. The premises were examined carefully, and only one suitable place could be found, an old disused outside lavatory at the back of the cafe, probably built towards the end of the last century and which had remained locked up for at least the past 20 years. Small and dark and damp and cramped and smelly, it could just about accommodate an officer and his equipment, and the triumphant Ferguson declared it perfect for the purpose.

The police technicians worked all night. The speakers were converted to microphones. Wires were led down the back of the building and into the old lavatory, where a wire recorder was set up, powered by a wire specially installed from the main fuse box, since there was no electricity laid on in that area, and everything was ready for action.

Next morning Mr. Ferguson returned and towered over the bemused Mario.

'This requires absolute discretion on everybody's part. It would be rather awkward for all concerned if it ever got out, wouldn't it?'

Mario's frantic nodding of the head was rewarded with a pat on the back. Mario could remember only too well the smell of the Canadian internment camp.

And so began what was to be called 'The Shite House Shift' by the participating policemen.

Every Saturday and Sunday, from round about noon till closing time some unfortunate police officer sat cold and cramped for four hours on a plank placed over the toilet seat in the old lavatory, headphones clamped on his ears, ready to switch on the recording mechanism at the first sound of conversation. Every hour another constable would pass to

retrieve the recorded spool, which presumably was taken off for analysis somewhere. Every four hours the policeman in the lavatory was relieved, emerging stiff and blue with the cold (it was the middle of winter), to ask Mario for a hot cup of coffee in the privacy of the back shop, and to curse the effing edjits who had thought the idea up.

Wendy Wood and her followers came and went and orated and conversed but it is doubtful if any useful information came over the wires. The occasional word could be made out, but what emerged from the recordings was mainly a rumble of incomprehensible conversation. During all this time the Hikers occasionally asked for some favourite record to be played, and complained quite bitterly at the length of time it was taking to repair the loudspeaker system.

Finally after six weeks, to the great relief of the participating policemen, the fruitless 'Shite House Shift' was called off, the wires were removed from the outside lavatory, the speakers were returned to their original condition and the upstairs customers could once more listen to Mario's music selection for their pleasure. During the period of the surveillance the Stone had been returned to Arbroath by the perpetrator, Ian Hamilton, who was later to become an eminent QC, and whether Wendy Wood was involved at all in the affair has never been known.

Five months later, official permission for Mario to work in the family business arrived from the Home Office. The application had been lodged the morning after Ferguson's visit. Tam's 6 pounds 10 a week stopped, but the big farmer was always welcome to the hospitality of The Savoy, in the form of a free fish supper, any time he cared to visit.

CHAPTER 20
Eddie

*I*n the west end of Glasgow, in a quiet street near the Botanic Gardens, there stands a graceful building of listed architectural worth. This building for the last 125 years or so has housed the Western Baths Club, a welcome oasis of rest and recreation for all those fortunate enough to be members. The membership is and always has been cosmopolitan and rich in variety, and has encompassed bookies, shopkeepers, actors, t.v. announcers, personalities from the nearby BBC studios, members of the professions, Catholic priests and Protestant ministers. Ethnic and religious background has never been a factor in the selection of membership. All that was required of prospective members was that they should measure up to a certain standard of behaviour and decorum and that they should be able to meet the relatively modest fees entailed by membership. The baths has gone through many vicissitudes in its long history, and came near to ruin in the seventies, when dilapidation and lack of funds drove it to the verge of bankruptcy. That it survived and prospered to

become one of the best equipped establishments of its kind in the country is due entirely to the efforts and vision of the present chairman, Mr Willie Mann, who steered it through the difficulties of that period and saved it from extinction.

In the eighties one of the longest serving members of the Western Baths was a certain doctor of medicine, Eddie Collier. A member since the end of the war, on Mondays, Wednesdays and Fridays, which were the gents days, Eddie could always be found there, from midday to late afternoon, going through his ritual like clockwork. This consisted of a swim in the pool, then a spell in the hot rooms and finally a shower. This was followed by the luxury of a long period in the warm, well-furnished dressing room, where, for hours on end, he would hold court in the company of a dozen or so members. A seat at Eddie's table was much sought after, for the conversation there was always stimulating and controversial, touching as it did on every conceivable subject, from topical matters to politics and religion.

Mario of The Savoy was also a regular visitor, and like Eddie, a long time member of the baths, since 1952, to be precise. The Western Baths had been Mario's second choice of club. In those years clubs in general were short of members, for the war years had depleted membership, and the reconstruction period that followed did not allow people much time for leisure activities. The Arlington Baths, a club near Charing Cross was canvassing for members; Mario applied for entry and was suitably proposed and seconded. He was promptly blackballed, not because of his Italian name, as he imagined he might have been, but because of his religion, Catholic. Religious affiliation was one of the questions asked on the application form of many institutions then: so as not to appear blatantly sectarian, some would ask only for the name of any school attended, which amounted to the same thing,

really. Stuff them, thought Mario, the members at the Arlington must be a real crummy bunch and considered himself well out of it. The name of the Western Baths was suggested to him, an immediate application was lodged, and Mario found himself accepted and very comfortably at home with the broad variety of members there.

Once a member, Mario was immediately attracted to Eddie's table, and to Eddie himself, a quiet unassuming Jewish bachelor about 10 years older than Mario, with a wide spectrum of interests, and always neatly but rather more poorly dressed than one would expect from a man in his profession. He had no immediate family and lived alone in a clean but sparsely furnished rented tenement flat in Garrioch Road. The friendship between the two grew over the years, and when Eddie retired from his post as an environmental health doctor with Rolls Royce in the late seventies he became a frequent visitor at Mario's home, where he was well liked by all the family.

In the early eighties Mario too retired from business and decided to spend much of the year in Majorca, where one of his daughters now lived, and thus his visits to the baths and his meetings with Eddie became irregular and less frequent.

In December 1987 Mario returned to Glasgow after an extended stay in Majorca. No sooner had he arrived from the airport than the phone rang.

'Hello, Uncle Mario, it's Frank,' This was his nephew, a young lawyer with a firm of Glasgow solicitors. 'I thought you might just have arrived. There's nothing wrong', thus pre-empting Mario's immediate concern. 'It's just that the procurator fiscal's office has been in touch with me to find out if you were the Mario Petri who lived in Milngavie about 15 years ago, and what your present address was. There should be a letter from them in your post.'

Mario found the letter and hurriedly tore it open. The

note stated that his friend Eddie had been found dead in his flat some days before. The funeral was to take place the very next morning in the Jewish cemetery at Maryhill, with a service in the synagogue there. Would he please come to the procurator's office at his earliest, a holograph will had been found, and he, Mario, was named in it as executor.

The funeral was sparsely attended as was the service in the little synagogue at the side of the cemetery, with two Rabbis, the Jewish undertakers, and a handful of friends from the Western Baths the only people present. One of the Rabbis approached Mario.

'You're Mr Petri, I'm told. I don't know why Mr Collier did not appoint one of his own kind as executor. However, if that was his wish, so be it. However, I must ask that if you come across any Jewish religious objects in his home you will hand them over to me.'

That afternoon, saddened at the death of his little friend, and deeply touched at the trust Eddie had placed in him, Mario sat in the fiscal's office and started to read Eddie's handwritten will. It was dated December 1974 and contained a request that his friend Mario Petri be appointed as executor of his will. After a few small bequests the remainder of the estate was to go to The Royal National Lifeboat Institute in Troon. The last line of the will read: 'I desire that on my demise my body be cremated.'

He looked at the fiscal.

'But he was buried this morning. Who made the funeral arrangements?'

The fiscal didn't know. 'Maybe the police could help you there.'

Mario thought for a minute, 'How do I go on from here?'

'This box was found in a desk in Dr Collier's home

with his will on top of it. He had no immediate relatives, so since you are the executor we have to open this box in your presence. Probably you will want your own solicitor to advise you as to how to proceed.'

A metal deed box was forced open. Inside it were some documents and bank books. Mario opened one, then another, added up some figures and took a deep breath.

'I think I'd better call my lawyer. I'm up to over £100,000 already.'

The deed box was taken to the lawyer's office, where the various documents and certificates were sorted out. The gross value of Eddie's assets, before deduction of debts and charges amounted to almost £400,000. But Mario's main consideration was the fact that, contrary to Eddie's stated wish, a burial and not a cremation had been carried out at the funeral. The police who had discovered the body were contacted. Who had given instructions for the burial? The police supposed that it had been the local Rabbi. Given that Eddie was Jewish and had no family, the body had been released to his synagogue. Did the Rabbi know of the contents of the will, or had it gone straight to the fiscal's office? Somebody surely must have known that Eddie wanted a cremation and not a burial?

Nobody seemed to be able to answer these questions. Mario phoned the Rabbi and explained his dilemma and was met with a tirade. 'Cremation is contrary to Jewish law,' spluttered the priest. 'No Jew would want to be cremated, and although he did not practise his religion Eddie would always be a Jew, and he must have been out of his mind to have written such a request.' Mario persisted. Did the Rabbi know of Eddie's request? 'It doesn't matter whether I knew or not. I would never allow a Jew to be cremated,' was the reply, and the conversation ended on a very sour note.

Mario explained his concern to the lawyer. The fact that his old friend had thought enough of him to have him settle his affairs touched Mario deeply, and he felt that he would not be doing his duty unless Eddie's wishes were carried out. The body must be disinterred and then cremated he insisted, and an advocate was consulted for an opinion.

Let Eddie lie where he is, was the judgement. Mario could not blame himself, for he had not known of Eddie's request until the burial had taken place. The synagogue may well have acted in good faith, without any knowledge of Eddie's wish, and even if they had seen the will and chosen to disregard his request, such a fact would be well nigh impossible to prove. Moreover, the body was now buried in the Jewish equivalent of consecrated ground, and the synagogue would fight tooth and nail any action to disinter the body and have it removed elsewhere. An action might in the end be successful, but it would certainly be acrimonious and might well seem to be racially motivated. Given the opposition it would certainly encounter, costs would be astronomical.

And the advice was repeated; let Eddie lie as he is.

The Jewish section at Maryhill Cemetery is a small wall-enclosed space at the southern end of the Catholic cemetery. The headstones were of modest size and quality, and as he stood over the fresh earth at his old friend's grave Mario decided that somehow his last (unwanted) resting place should be specially noted. A magnificent and very expensive polished granite slab engraved with Eddie's name was placed as headstone over the full extent of the grave. It stood out like a Taj Mahal in the very modest surroundings, as if to emphasise that Eddie was really out of place there. With the passing of the years, however, it has been noted that many of the surrounding headstones have been replaced by markers

equal to, if not greater than, Eddie's in splendour. On his yearly visits to the grave Mario is beset by a feeling of guilt that somehow he has failed his friend.

At the Royal National Lifeboat Institute station in Troon harbour a brass plaque acknowledges Eddie's bequest.

CHAPTER 21
The Misfits

*T*he imposingly named Queen's Arcade was a rather dingy covered passageway which connected Cowcaddens Street with Sauchiehall Street via Stow Street and Wemyss Street. It entered into Renfrew Street where the Hospitality Inn stands now, and continued across and through what is now Marks and Spencers into Sauchiehall Street. It boasted of a fine variety of shops of all classes. At the Stow Street end stood Crockett's the ironmonger where one could buy anything from a pin to an anvil. Next to it was a small off-license, then came Da Prato's, the Italian delicatessen, then a couple of pubs, one of which, The Arcade Bar, had the unsavoury reputation of being the roughest drinking den in the Cowcaddens. Masters' butcher and fishmonger shop had a prominent frontage in the Arcade. It sold fish, bacon, eggs and various meats, all labelled as 'seconds' whatever that might have meant, but since the prices

were almost half of those charged elsewhere, the place did a roaring trade. In those days of food rationing not much attention was paid to such niceties as food hygiene and consumer protection, and the idea of a regulation making it necessary to label food products with a sell-by date was still to be born. One wonders what the incidence of salmonella (and worse) was amongst the customers of the place.

Occasionally Masters' would advertise a batch of haddock or whiting seconds at knock-down prices, and these would be snapped up immediately by Mario of the nearby Savoy Cafe for sale to his drunken night-time clientele. Steeped for a while in a mixture of salt water and vinegar, the seconds would lose the characteristic phosphorescent sheen of decomposing fish, and when fried in hot dripping, the temperature of which would effectively kill off any latent noxious organisms, the end product would look no different from a fresher and more wholesome piece of fish. The taste, akin to a pungently flavoured piece of dried cardboard, was another matter, but since The Savoy's late night customers were hardly possessed of a discerning palate, such a consideration was of no importance.

Then, at the end of a nondescript row of shoe and bric-a-brac shops, came The Camp Bar in Renfrew Street, a pub which must have given The Arcade Bar a good run for its money for the title of the toughest drinking place in the area. The continuation of the Arcade across Renfrew Street and into Sauchiehall Street offered a higher class type of retail outlet; a Monte Harris shirt shop, an HMV gramophone record shop, a bespoke shoe shop and finally two Malcolm Campbell fruit and flower shops at each corner on Sauchiehall Street.

But without a doubt the most famous establishment in the Arcade was The West End Misfits, a new and second-hand gents outfitters and dress hire shop. The name of the shop was

itself a misfit, since it wasn't in the West End, and since it boasted of being able to clothe anyone of any size, 'Misfits' didn't seem quite apt either. The proprietors were three Cockney brothers, Frank, Maurice and Benny Goodman, who had brought the name of their London shop with them at the time of their diaspora to Glasgow in the immediate post-war years.

The move from London had been made necessary by the fact that a salvo of German V1 and V2 missiles had obliterated their premises together with several surrounding streets in the last months of the war. In Scotland the brunt of Luftwaffe air raids had fallen on Clydebank; Glasgow city centre had suffered little or no bomb damage and offered many thriving retail areas, and so the brothers had come north to re-establish their business. Trade was booming in the city. Factories were working full blast to repair the ravages of war, everyone had money in their pockets, but with everything rationed there was nothing to spend it on apart from pubs, cinemas and dance halls. Clothing was especially severely rationed. The few clothing coupons issued to each person for a year could barely buy a couple of shirts, and so the West End Misfits, with its vast stocks of second-hand clothing of all sizes could barely cope with the volume of trade.

The three brothers divided the work amongst them in accordance to each one's qualities. Frank and Maurice were the smooth tongued and persuasive salesmen, whilst Benny, exuding trust, confidence and charisma, was the buyer of stock. Part of the purchasing strategy was a diligent perusal of the death notices in the *Glasgow Herald* and other local papers. Benny would see to it that the area in which the bereavement had taken place was circulated with pamphlets offering to buy male clothes of all kinds in good condition, and then a few days later, a fistful of pound notes in hand, the houses in the

district, including of course that of the bereaved, were visited. The yield from the bereaved households was always very good, and consisted often of the best quality pre-war suits, unworn and stored away during a possibly long terminal illness, and purchased from a disconsolate widow by a suitably sympathetic Benny at rock bottom prices.

Benny seldom set foot in the family shop. He was a free-ranging soul who could not bear the constraints of four shop walls and when not on some purchasing errand spent all his time wandering from pub to pub in search of conviviality and any business opportunity that might be forthcoming. The Savoy was his favourite haunt. There he would spend hours chatting, exchanging jokes and betting on the horses with one or other of the bookies always to be found there, amongst whom he was a great favourite, since he bet heavily and never seemed to have any luck in picking a winner.

One day as he sat awaiting the results of a race, he was approached by Peter McNulty the taxi driver, with the offer of the sale of an overcoat. It was no ordinary coat. It was a large and beautifully tailored article made from the best crombie cloth with plush satin linings and a velvet collar, obviously worth not only a lot of money but also a couple of years' supply of clothing coupons. Benny snapped it up without asking too much about its origins. A reassurance from the seller that it was not stolen sufficed. Peter was known to be a bit of a headcase, but his honesty had never been called into question (this was just before the affair of the golden sovereigns, told in chapter 7). The magnificent coat was placed on prominent display in the shop with a high price tag. Frank and Maurice were not in a hurry to sell it. It gave a touch of class to the window display.

In those days theatre and cinema attendance was probably at its peak. Apart from the wireless there was no

other form of entertainment or distraction from the drabness of immediate post-war life. It was certainly the era of the big touring dance bands, Ambrose and his orchestra, Geraldo and his orchestra. Lou Praeger and his band, Ted Heath and his band, Henry Hall and the BBC Dance Orchestra, Nat Gonella and his band, Ray Noble and his orchestra, all these were household names whose regular visits to the city centre theatres and dance halls were eagerly awaited and booked out months in advance by an avid public.

Not least in this list of dance orchestras was The Lew Stone Band. This was a popular top class London outfit with a variety of gifted musicians and singers, amongst whom was the nationally famous drummer Max Bacon, a giant of a man with a pleasantly rasping singing voice whose solo act featured prominently in the band's repertoire. At the time of these events the orchestra had just finished a two week appearance at The Empire and had been celebrating the beginning of a week's rest period. To mark the occasion Max had given a party at his usual digs in Garnethill where the wine flowed more freely than usual since there was to be no work the next day. As the time of his departure on the night sleeper to London approached, the jovial drummer was well advanced into a state of alcoholic fuzziness. A taxi was called to take him and his belongings to Central Station, where he was duly loaded onto the night sleeper by a helpful Peter McNulty, who was on his last job of the night. Next morning the taxi driver was agreeably surprised to find a magnificent overcoat on the floor of his cab, and Max Bacon arrived in London minus his velvet collared crombie without the slightest idea as to where he might have left it. A phone call to the digs in Glasgow produced no results. With no desire to let it be known that he had drunk himself into forgetfulness by pursuing the matter further, Max resigned himself to the loss

of his coat, knowing that the value of it was covered by insurance, even though the coat could not be soon replaced because of the lack of clothing coupons.

A month or so passed and the Lew Stone Band returned for a fortnight's visit to Glasgow. The crombie coat in the window of The West End Misfits, as yet unsold, still formed the centrepiece of the display. On Wednesdays and Saturdays, matinee days, Max Bacon made a point of having a meal of fish and chips at The Savoy, where, since his visits were always in the late afternoon, there was no possibility of eating anything but the best quality fish. On one of these visits Benny happened to be sitting, regaling his company with his jokes and stories. He was a marvellous raconteur, using his slight Cockney accent to advantage, and Max could not but join in the general enjoyment of Benny's tales. From obviously similar backgrounds, pleasantries were exchanged and common haunts and backgrounds in London established. Max Bacon's profession needed no introduction, but when Benny introduced himself as being in the clothing business, the musician's thoughts turned to the lost overcoat, as yet unreplaced given the lack of clothing coupons.

'I've got just the very thing for you,' enthused Benny, 'a beautiful piece of cloth. You won't find any better in Saville Row. Just your size too, I imagine. Second-hand but better than new. No coupons, and for you we'll make a special price. Come and see it tomorrow.'

And Benny hurried off to the Arcade, where, in anticipation of the musician's visit. his brothers promptly added 15 per cent to the already inflated price of the coat.

Max Bacon took one startled look at the coat on display in the shop window, said not a word, but turned on his heel to return 10 minutes later with a policeman in tow and confronted the mystified Goodman brothers with a

demand for the immediate return of his coat, with muttered threats and accusations of theft and reset. His ownership established, the musician retreated triumphant, proudly wearing the lost coat. The brothers managed to convince the police of their innocence in the matter. They had been taken in by the person who had sold them the coat, they claimed. The fact that they had exhibited it in plain view in their window should be proof enough of their good faith, they continued. Had they anything to hide, the coat could have been disposed of long ago privately. Where had they got the coat? They made a great show of going through invoices and records. 'It must have been part of a job lot from some unknown source', they concluded, and in view of the delicacy of the situation the police let the matter drop. They knew full well the unwritten law that prevailed in such a neighbourhood. If you don't want the roof to fall in on you, thou shalt not shop your neighbour, especially if he is as well liked as Peter McNulty was.

It took a disgruntled Benny at least a day to recover from the shock of the loss of the five pounds he had paid Peter McNulty for the coat.

CHAPTER 22

Vincent

*T*he game of chess was one of the two great overriding passions in Vincent's life. Someone once said that chess was too serious to be a pastime and too frivolous to be an occupation, but to Vincent it seemed to be literally a matter of life or death. A good part of his day was spent hunched over a board oblivious to all else as he analysed the complexities of an opponent's Sicilian Defence answer to his Ruy Lopez gambit. On these occasions his mind was closed to everything except the permutations on the squares in front. Should he transpose into a Nimzovitch attack? But then his adversary might go to a Petroff defence, which Vincent always found very difficult to cope with. Should he bring Alekhine into play? But then he might be faced with a Falkbeer counter gambit which would expose his own Queen's pawn weakness. These matters were considered very carefully, until, forced by

the possibility of a time loss as measured on his omnipresent double faced chess clock, a meaningless move would be made, to the consternation of his equally engrossed opponent who would thus be driven to frantic brain searching in an attempt to discover the supposedly sinister motive behind Vincent's unexpected move.

Many of these games were played on a table conveniently provided in a secluded corner of The Savoy for his chess playing customers by the owner Mario, who during quiet periods permitted himself the waste of an hour or so in pitting his wits against any of the customers who fancied their chances against him. Vincent was a daily visitor to the table, and so that his games could be played strictly according to the rules, he always brought with him his chess clock, a finely engraved Ingersoll inherited from a long dead grandfather.

The second great passion in Vincent's life was the cinema. The influence of the cinema on the populace in the early thirties is impossible to exaggerate. The newly invented 'talkies' had brought sound and dialogue to the flickering images on the screen, and cinema-goers in their thousands upon thousands flocked to the picture houses to hear their favourite stars speak their dialogue in the strange new accents of the USA. Viewers sat transfixed as Jolson, Gable and Cagney spoke their lines in an American accent which was gradually becoming comprehensible to audiences who until then had known only the sound of their own local Glasgow patter, and who sat open-mouthed as Garbo was heard to speak for the first time.

'Garbo Talks!' shrieked the posters, and people queued for hours to hear her ask for a whisky in a throaty whisper. Ronald Colman entranced the ladies as he made love in impeccable English to an equally impeccably accented Elissa Landi, and Gary Cooper held his audiences hypnotised as he

spoke in a flat western drawl and challenged the baddie to draw his gun.

Vincent's screen idol was the suave and sinister George Raft, whose dress and mannerisms he attempted to copy, down to the rolling of a coin along the backs of the fingers. No silver dollar was available to Vincent, but he made do with a half-crown piece, with which he made a passable imitation of his screen hero as he waited for his chess opponent to make a move.

Vincent also had to find time to earn a living, which he did somewhat grudgingly by dispensing ice-cream wafers and pokey hats in his nearby father's cafe on the occasions when the long suffering parent could drag him away from his dream worlds of chess and cinema. Vincent was Italian born and had come to Glasgow as a child with one of the hundreds of Italian families who had emigrated to Scotland immediately after World War I, and in those days if you were Italian you were either in fish and chips or ice cream to make a living, a tradition which has in many cases survived to the present day.

As has been stated many a time in these stories, The Savoy stood on the fringes of a very rough district and from time to time undesirables from the area had to be barred from entering the premises. One day as Mario sat watching a particularly engrossing game between Vincent and another chess devotee, the door opened and one of the many banes of his life walked up to the table. Norie Smith was what the police called 'a real bad bastard', a thin foxed-faced weasel of a man with shifty close set eyes, pasty pimply skin and fingers heavily stained with the nicotine from his chain smoked Woodbines. He had never worked in his life and scrounged around the Cowcaddens preying on small shopkeepers and prostitutes to augment his weekly 'Broo' money. The former considered it worth the occasional two bob levy not to have

their windows smashed during the night, and the unfortunates among the latter who did not have the protection of a pimp reluctantly paid so as not to have their faces cut up by the razor carried by Smith in an inside pocket. This razor was also a threat to the buskers who entertained the cinema and theatre queues in Sauchiehall Street, and who also contributed to his income so as not to have their routine disrupted by a fracas. He was also very popular indeed amongst the street news vendors of the district who did not relish having their pavement stock of papers urinated upon in the event of a refusal by them. The police of course regularly picked him up and confiscated his weapon, but a couple of nights in the cells only served to rest him up a bit, and razors were cheaply obtained.

He had been long barred from entering the portals of The Savoy and had often felt the weight of Big Steve's hands as he attempted to avoid the banishment. He did persist in entering from time to time during the day when no doorman stood guard, but this was only to annoy, for he knew full well that he would be shown the door in no uncertain fashion.

He stood by the chess table. Mario got to his feet.

'Come on, get out. You know you're barred here. Unless you want to talk to your friends over there,' and he gestured to a neighbouring table occupied by some of Jimmy McKay's runners who had begun to take an interest in the proceedings. Since Smith was also given to pestering the bookie's punters, the runners would have dearly loved an excuse to break his arms.

Smith looked around and spat on the floor.

'Fuck you all,' he intoned and identified an object on which to vent his spleen. Concentrating on the chess board, Vincent had been oblivious to all this and could barely comprehend what was happening. As quick as a flash the

hooligan picked up the chess clock and smashed it to bits on the hard terrazzo floor and then ran into the street. Vincent sadly picked up the pieces.

'Why did he have to do that? My grandfather gave me it a long time ago,' he said as he went off inconsolably to his work in the family shop, leaving a game unfinished for the first time in his life. He was also angry with himself, because he was sure that his hero Raft would have reacted differently to the event and that he himself could have done something to prevent the loss of his beloved clock. He visualized the scene as it would have been on the cinema screen. Raft would have flicked the omnipresent silver dollar into his left hand, then with his right would have reached out, caught the precious clock in mid-air, and laid low the offender with a mighty blow and continued nonchalantly with his Ponziani opening. But he himself had done nothing, just sat there open-mouthed as his precious possession was destroyed. His self esteem sank very low.

With time the hurt of the incident faded. If anything, it had had a salutary effect in bringing Vincent to grips with reality. He still enjoyed his visits to the cinema, but he discarded the George Raft mannerisms, with the exception of the juggled silver coin, a habit which seemed to focus his concentration. He still continued with his games of chess at the table in The Savoy, but more and more time was now devoted to the furtherance of the family business.

The middle and late thirties were times of turbulent events in the world. Civil war was raging in Spain, Mussolini had invaded Abysinnia and the shadow of Hitler was beginning to fall over the countries of Europe. The writing was plain on the wall for those who wished to read it: a war was inevitable and in it Italy would be the enemy of Britain. Vincent's father was in these matters a far-seeing man. He

remembered only too well the upheaval of the 1914-18 war and the stories told by Italian civilians who had been imprisoned in that war by the enemy, Austria. Could the same thing happen in Britain now that war with his homeland seemed to be on the cards? He sought the counsel of a cousin who had set himself up in business many years ago in Dublin. Southern Ireland under De Valera had long since declared itself neutral in any possible European conflict and according to the cousin offered many business opportunities for anyone willing to work hard. Most important, the Irish in Dublin were all Catholic, and by and large Italians were well-liked and not subjected to the insults and taunts sometimes levelled at them in a sectarian Glasgow. A decision was made and preparations set in motion for a transfer of the family to Dublin. In this Vincent played an important part. In 1939 he had reached the age of 25 and although chess and cinema still played an important role in his life they had been relegated to their proper position as pastimes and he worked constructively with his father towards the proposed move across the sea to Ireland.

In September of that year Britain went to war with Germany, but Mussolini made no move and Italy stayed out. In June 1940 all had been concluded for the move to Dublin, and on the 6th of that month Vincent embarked on the Glasgow-Dublin boat: his father, with a few loose ends to tie up in the sale of the business, was to follow a fortnight later. On the 10th June Italy declared war on Britain. Vincent's father, now an enemy alien, suffered the fate he had feared and foreseen and was arrested and interned. Ten days later he was dead at the bottom of the Atlantic ocean, entombed in the ill-fated prison ship *Arandora Star* sunk by a German torpedo off the coast of Ireland where he had hoped to find sanctuary.

On his way to the docks Vincent had asked the taxi

driver to stop by The Savoy so that he could say farewell to his friend Mario. They chatted for a while, shook hands and Mario escorted him to the door for a final goodbye. Vincent got into the taxi, and as he prepared to close the door he noticed a figure slouched up against the wall. He paused for a moment, got out and approached.

'Remember me? Do you remember the clock you broke?'

With the spirit of George Raft now alive within him, he grabbed Norie Smith by the lapels and shaking him like a rag doll, threw him violently to the ground. Resisting the urge to kick him, Vincent returned to the taxi and opened the door. Smith jumped up drooling with rage. He drew his razor, opening it with a well-practised flicking motion, and rushed at his attacker. Vincent side-stepped, forced the razor wielding hand into the door of the taxi and slammed it several times into Smith's fingers. The razor embedded itself into its owner's hand and broke off there, leaving Smith screaming with pain, blood pouring out of a deep gash in his palm. Vincent looked impassively at him, gave a last wave to Mario, and motioned the taxi on. Mario let a few moments pass as Smith sat bleeding and screaming on the pavement, then leisurely went inside to call the police. They knew the victim only too well and decided not to waste any time in investigating the matter. Smith was bundled into an ambulance and literally dumped at the doors of the Royal Infirmary where the broken razor blade was removed and the hand stitched up. It healed badly and crookedly, leaving him with paralysed fingers and a twisted wrist. His razor wielding days were over. He lived on for many years, a shambling bent beggar with a twisted hand, relying on the occasional compassionate handout from the very persons he had terrorised in years gone by.

Some 55 years have passed. The scene is The Bonanza

Playa Hotel in Majorca and Mario, long retired and very much older and withered, has just sauntered into the hotel lounge from his holiday apartment some yards down the road to enjoy a relaxing drink. At one end of the lounge there are a few green baize-covered games tables. One or two of the tables have chess sets ready for the use of patrons. At one of them he notices a solitary figure, obviously working out chess problems. A silver coin is slowly being rolled between old and gnarled arthritic fingers. A old memory stirs and slowly takes shape in Mario's head and he sits down in front of the old man at the table.

'Hello Vincent. Long, long time no see. How about a quick King's pawn gambit?'

CHAPTER 23

The Clappertons

At the beginning of the 20th Century, Glasgow, the second city of the Empire, could proudly lay claim to some of the finest public parks in the world: Queen's Park, Rouken Glen, Linn Park, Pollock Park, The Botanic Gardens; all these were extensive and beautifully kept oases of parkland in the middle of the dark and grimy tenements of the day. In them the good citizens of the city could wander at will, breathing in the sweet scent of the countryside and admiring the well laid out and beautifully maintained paths and flower beds. At weekends the parks would fill with families dressed in their Sunday best, with proud parents pushing prams or leading children by the hand, the women in their best dresses and the men in suits or blazers and wearing the latest model in snap brim hats at the approved angle as seen in the latest John Gilbert movie.

To match these parks, the city also boasted of some

excellent public golf courses. These 'Corporation' courses, Littlehill, Linn Park, Deaconsbank, Lethamhill, Clydebank and Knightswood, were as well-tended as the parks and offered a round of golf for sixpence to those, and they were by far in the majority in those days, who could not afford the luxury of membership at some of the more select private courses which surrounded the city.

Young Johnny Clapperton played regularly on the corporation golf courses of Glasgow. His favourite was Littlehill, firstly because it presented a stiff test of anybody's golfing abilities and secondly because the stop for the bus to take you there was in the Cowcaddens, just a few steps along from his place of work, the Maitland Street police station. The bus stop was handy too for Mario of The Savoy and Louie Beretti, a young fish fryer from a nearby restaurant both of whom had also been well bitten by the golfing bug. The three, the rookie policeman and the two young Italians played together at least once a week. In 1935 no one ever thought of any means of transportation other than tram or bus, so the Cowcaddens bus stop was the pre-arranged meeting place. There they would meet whoever was making up a foursome for that particular game and they would set off, eager to break par with the hickory-shafted clubs then in vogue.

Occasionally Jimmy McKay the bookie made up the four, and on those occasions the journey would be made in style in his motor car. Possession of a motor car was then a luxury reserved for the fortunate few and Jimmy's served as a status symbol so that his punters could know that he had enough wherewithal to cover all their bets and that their money was safe with him. His car in 1935 was a modest bull-nosed Morris Oxford; the white Rolls Royce mentioned in another story lay far in the future.

Johnny Clapperton lived with his younger sister Isobel

in a tenement flat in Maryhill. Orphaned at an early age, they had been raised by an aunt and when she too died in her early sixties they continued to live in the flat which had been their home since the death of their parents. The aunt had raised them strictly but lovingly and they had matured into responsible adults with a sense of duty and a desire to make something of themselves in life. Well-built, healthy and strong, Johnny had decided on a career as a policeman and at 19 started his training at the Police Academy in Tullyallan. On completion of his course he was posted to the Maitland Street station and there he had acquired his present circle of friends and golfing companions.

Attracted to all kinds of physical activities and with an intense interest in flying, he trained two evenings a week at Prestwick airfield as a cadet in the Royal Auxiliary Air Force. In the summer, these evenings would be made the occasion for a golf outing with his Littlehill companions on St Cuthberts, a golf course adjoining the airfield. The journey from Glasgow was always made by train even if Jimmy McKay was one of the party, since a return ticket was only one and ninepence and the trains were punctual. A 1935 vintage Morris could not guarantee you a round trip of 60 or so miles without the spectre of some kind of mechanical hiccup or puncture. The airfield runway ran closely parallel to the course's fourth fairway, and the golf was at times temporarily forgotten at the sight of planes taking off and landing so close by. Aeroplanes were still a novelty then. The drone of an aeroplane engine was enough to stop people in their tracks, heads tilted back and finger pointing aloft at this latest mechanical marvel. For the adventurous, the weekend thrill consisted of a tram ride to Renfrew Airport, where for five shillings you could buy a bumpy 15-minute hop at 2000 feet in a rickety biplane, an event to be boasted about for days afterwards.

These were the days of the Schneider Trophy races, the much vaunted air races between the best pilots and aeroplanes that Europe and America had to offer, and for Britain the testing ground for what was to become the Spitfire interceptor fighter. These prototypes were used as trainers for RAF pilots, and the sight of these graceful monoplanes swooping and soaring above the Ayrshire beaches, sometimes alone, sometimes in tight, perfectly maintained formation, was a sight to behold. For the golfers, the fact that their pal Johnny was one of the pilots raised the esteem in which he was already held by them.

Louie was much attracted by Johnny's sister Isobel, who, on leaving school had started work in a dressmaker's shop at the Clydebank end of Dumbarton Road. The attraction was mutual, much to Johnny's satisfaction, for he thought highly of Louie and reckoned that she would be hard put to find a better partner than the hard-working serious minded young Italian.

There were not many casual relationships between the sexes in those days. If you kept company with a respectable girl for any length of time then certain things were expected. In this case, however, there was one great obstacle in any proposed road to the altar. Louie was Italian-born and the only son of parents who barely spoke English and who persisted in holding on to the traditions of their native land, even though the motherland had been unable to offer them a life worth living and had forced them to emigrate to richer and more progressive shores.

In the mid-thirties there were about 1500 Italian-born families in Scotland, most of whom had arrived immediately after the 1914-18 war to settle mainly in the Glasgow-Edinburgh corridor. Many of these families came from southern parts of Italy and were much more set in their

traditional ways than were the immigrants from the more northern parts of the country. They formed a perfect background for the activities of a southern-Italian phenomenon of those days, the 'ruffiana'. A modern dictionary will translate the word as 'procuress', but to the early Italian immigrants it was simply a title given to an arranger of marriages, a marriage broker. Glasgow had one well-known and successful 'ruffiana', and it is safe to say that the vast majority of Italian weddings which took place in the thirties in Scotland were arranged matches, the results of encounters organised by this lady. She visited family after family and took note of persons of marriageable age. Their background would be observed, economic standing judged and meetings of candidates and parents arranged. With the latter a suitable fee for her services would be agreed, usually with the female's parents, for it was of the maximum importance that a girl be well married and a father would be prepared to pay well for a satisfactory union. Her work stopped with the introduction however; from then on it was the job of the parents to bring pressure to bear and this was almost always successful, for what dutiful son or daughter would go against a parent's wishes in such important matters?

She worked hard and long seeking out a suitable match for the son of the Berettis. A better prospective husband would be difficult to find. Not much money perhaps, but honest and hardworking and a perfect match for someone with the ambition to spur him on to better things. The young man would have none of it. Nubile though the girls presented to him may have been, his eyes were only for Isobel and despite howls of anguish and recrimination from his parents began to make plans to marry the girl of his own choice. The year was 1939 and momentous and sinister events were taking place in Europe, with the rise of Hitler, the Spanish Civil War

and Mussolini's invasion of Ethiopia paving the way for the eventual outbreak of war.

Momentous events were taking place in the world of golf as well. Hickory-shafted clubs were now becoming obsolete, supplanted by the much more efficient and reliable steel-shafted products, and Johnny Clapperton was the first in his group to buy a set. But not just an ordinary set. He had managed to acquire a matched set of Tommy Armour steel shafts, beautifully crafted implements, the wooden clubs with persimmon heads and the irons hollow forged to give a perfect balance and sweet spot. Also, they had oval grips, something never seen before in a golf club and which in later years were to become illegal because of the advantage they gave in lining up a shot. Mario and Louie and Jimmy McKay literally drooled with envy and looked forward to the day when they could see Johnny in action with his new implements.

But that day was never to come. In the August of 1939, exactly one month before Hitler's invasion of Poland, Johnny was called to full active service with the RAF. He took his farewell of a tearful sister and solemn friends, His new unused Tommy Armour clubs were entrusted to the safekeeping of his brother-in-law to be, Louie. On the 3rd September Britain declared war on Germany and two days later, Johnny, on the first reconnaissance flight of the war over enemy territory, was shot down and killed, the first RAF casualty of the war.

Louie attempted to console a heartbroken Isobel. A date was set for their wedding in June of the following year, but in that month Mussolini declared war on Britain and Louie, now an enemy alien, was immediately arrested and put on a prison ship, the *Arandora Star*, for deportation to Canada. He survived the sinking of that vessel, only to be put promptly onto another, the *Dunera*, which was to deposit him two

months later thousands of miles away in Australia.

Bereft of the two persons she most loved, Isobel tried to find solace in hard work. Because of the introduction of clothes rationing the dress shop had no need of assistants, so she joined both a local ambulance unit and ARP station. She could no longer bear to live in the Maryhill flat with all its happy memories and found accommodation in a flat on the outskirts of Clydebank, where she prayed nightly that the war would soon end and that she could be reunited with her beloved Louie. One night in March 1941 the Luftwaffe mounted a massive air-raid on the docks and factories of Clydebank, and in the process destroyed row upon row of tenements. As she was trying to bring help to people trapped in the wreckage a burning tenement collapsed on the ambulance, killing Isobel outright.

One year after the end of the war Louie returned to Glasgow to pick up the ruins of his shattered life. He never married. He is now elderly and retired and so has plenty of time for his regular visits to Isobel's neatly tended grave in the St Kentigern cemetery. He has plenty of time too for golf, as have his two old friends from pre-war days. The 'Corporation' courses are not visited now, the three are life members of a well-known course on the outskirts of Glasgow, where they meet three times a week. Not always to play golf however; the advancing years have taken their toll of body and bones, but if the weather is particularly good the trio go out for a few holes. On these occasions Louie tees off with a well-worn but beautifully kept set of old fashioned steel-shafted clubs with distinctive oval grips.

EPILOGUE

ost of the protagonists of these stories have long since gone to meet their maker, but some of them live on. Vincent, bent and stooped and gnarled, his arthritic fingers barely capable of lifting a chess piece, but with a brain still capable of analysing a Ruy Lopez gambit, has returned to live in Glasgow. Sam Corti is over 90 now, and tends to be a bit confused as to which army he served in during the war. Jimmy McKay is about the same age, but with an active mind which tends to make the sum lost in a Caserta Bank more than keep pace with inflation in the telling of his war-time exploits. Louie of 'The Clappertons', is now well over 80, quiet and reserved, and visits his golf course regularly in the summer. If the weather is good he plays a few holes, after which he meticulously cleans and polishes his oval-gripped golf clubs.

Detective Chief Inspector Joe Beattie, who started his career in the 'Betty' case, is miraculously still alive, despite the

illness which terminated his investigation into the Bible John murders and which has aged him prematurely. His thought processes however are unimpaired and he is a mine of information about life in the old Cowcaddens.

Mario of The Savoy too soldiers on. Slightly stooped, but still sprightly, he loves to walk the streets of the Glasgow he once knew so well. The old Cowcaddens of these stories no longer exists. Although the Glasgow city centre has remained relatively unchanged over the last 50 years, the area north of Renfrew Street has altered completely, even down to the road pattern. The Savoy and the tenement block in which it stood were demolished in 1971. The Royal Scottish Academy of Music and Drama stands exactly on the corner site of The Savoy and a large hotel, the Hospitality Inn, has been built where the bookies' runners once used to operate. 'The Brothers' pub, The McGregor, is long gone and the site on which it stood is now a criss-cross of ramps leading off and on to the M8 motorway. Of the other pubs mentioned in the stories only the Atholl Arms remains and beside it, a short distance away from the magnificent Royal Concert Hall, the Catholic Truth Society shop where Mario purchased his 'Holy Oil' carries on dispensing its aids to piety.

A modern passport office stands where big Emma held a hostile crowd at bay. Willie Dickie's Theatre Royal is still there, but the maze of mean streets behind have vanished to make way for the Scottish Television studios, which have also swallowed up Patterson's garage where Peter McNulty worked. Close by, the tenement where Betty was brutally murdered still stands, and a modern St Andrew's ambulance headquarters has been built where Tosh the housebreaker's house used to be.

The Maitland Street Police Station has been replaced by a high-rise block of modern flats; the patrolling beat men have vanished from the pavements and the police whistle has

given way to radio communication and the cellular phone.

The slum tenements of the area have all been demolished, and a good thing too. Dirty, mean and dingy the old Cowcaddens may well have been, but households as clean and neat and as well-ordered as any in the more affluent parts of the city were once to be found in it. It pulsed with life and character, neighbourliness and individuality; all of which are fast disappearing in the modern Glasgow of sanitised and amorphous shopping malls, of ersatz pizza parlours, lookalike wine bars and standardised eating places. The new Cowcaddens is now simply a place of featureless, soulless glass and steel structures which could equally be at home in a score of modern European cities.

And what of the descendants of the families who lived in those mean tenements? They now are housed in the modern peripheral estates of Easterhouse, Drumchapel and Pollock. They are perhaps less fortunate than their predecessors in the Cowcaddens, for they have no Renfrew Street to cross over into that other world. They are isolated in their modern-day squalor while the heart of the city beats far away from them.